ALBERT EINSTEIN

THE GIANT OF 20TH CENTURY SCIENCE

Judy L. Hasday

Enslow Publishers, Inc.
40 Industrial Road
Box 398
Berkeley Heights, NJ 07922
USA

PO Box 38
Aldershot
Hants GU12 6BP
UK

http://www.enslow.com

"There is probably no physicist living today whose name has become so widely known as that of Albert Einstein."

—Professor S. Arrhenius

In memory of Patricia Heather Burns.
Dear friend and colleague, you will be deeply missed.

Library of Congress Cataloging-in-Publication Data

Hasday, Judy L., 1957–
Albert Einstein : the giant of 20th century science / Judy L. Hasday.
v. cm. — (Nobel Prize-winning scientists)
Includes bibliographical references and index.
Contents: The prize—An unremarkable youth—Switzerland: an oasis in Europe—A tenuous start for an improbable genius—The miracle year of 1905—Among the scientific elite— An outsider in Berlin—Scientist, intellectual, and advocate for peace.
ISBN 0-7660-2185-8
1. Einstein, Albert, 1879-1955—Juvenile literature. 2. Physicists—Biography—Juvenile literature. [1. Einstein, Albert, 1879-1955. 2. Physicists. 3. Scientists. 4. Nobel Prizes—Biography.] I. Title. II. Series.
QC16.E5H37 2004
530'.092—dc22

2003015335

Printed in the United States of America

10 9 8 7 6 5 4 3 2 1

To Our Readers:
We have done our best to make sure all Internet Addresses in this book were active and appropriate when we went to press. However, the author and the publisher have no control over and assume no liability for the material available on those Internet sites or on other Web sites they may link to. Any comments or suggestions can be sent by e-mail to comments@enslow.com or to the address on the back cover.

Illustration Credits: © The Nobel Foundation, p. 5; ArtToday.com, pp. 9, 22, 51, 60, 106; Enslow Publishers, Inc., pp. 30, 77, 86; Library of Congress, pp. 99, 112.

Cover Illustration: Corel Corporation (background); Courtesy of the Archives, California Institute of Technology (foreground).

Contents

The Nobel Prize

Every year since its founding in 1901, the Nobel Prize has been awarded to individuals who have distinguished themselves in the fields of physiology or medicine, physics, chemistry, literature, and peace. (In 1968 a prize for economics was added.) The prize is named for Alfred Nobel, a Swede born in Stockholm in 1833, who grew up to become a successful chemist, manufacturer, and businessman.

Nobel began experimenting with ways to make nitroglycerine safer for practical use. Eventually he found a way to mix nitroglycerine with silica and make a paste. He could then shape the paste into a stick that could be placed in holes drilled in rocks. He patented this creation in 1867 and named it dynamite. In order to detonate the dynamite sticks, Nobel also invented a blasting cap that could be ignited by burning a fuse. The invention of dynamite, along with equipment like the diamond drilling crown and the pneumatic drill, significantly reduced the expenses associated with many types of construction work.

Soon Nobel's dynamite and blasting caps were in great demand. Nobel proved to be an astute businessman, establishing companies and laboratories throughout the world. He also continued to experiment with other chemical inventions and held more than 350 patents in his lifetime.

Alfred Nobel did not narrow his learning just to scientific knowledge. His love of literature and poetry prompted him to write his own works, and his social conscience kept him interested in peace-related issues.

When Nobel died on December 10, 1896, and his will was read, everyone was surprised to learn that he left instructions that the accumulated fortune from his companies and business ventures (estimated at more than $3 million U.S.) was to be used to award prizes in physics, chemistry, physiology or medicine, literature, and peace.

In fulfilling Alfred Nobel's will, the Nobel Foundation was established in order to oversee the funds left by Nobel and to coordinate the work of the prize-awarding institutions. Nobel prizes are presented every December 10, the anniversary of Alfred Nobel's death.

THE PRIZE

Albert Einstein is recognized as one of the most gifted intellects the world has ever known. In a relatively brief period of time (about fifteen years), Einstein forever changed the way people thought about space, time, and gravitation. Today, his very name is synonymous with the term "genius." How, then, could Albert Einstein—who arguably contributed more than any other scientist since Sir Isaac Newton to our modern vision of physical reality—not be awarded the Nobel Prize? Despite his many accomplishments, Einstein was rejected as a Nobel winner for eleven years (1910–1921).

Ironically, Einstein's first nomination in 1910 came from Wilhelm Ostwald, a professor of physical chemistry whom Einstein had contacted nine years earlier, inquiring about working as Ostwald's assistant. Ostwald never replied, and there has always been speculation as to whether he even remembered the early contact. Ostwald based his nomination on Einstein's special theory of relativity, and resubmitted Einstein's name on two more occasions.

In fact, Einstein was nominated for the Nobel Prize in Physics by various colleagues a total of eight times before he was finally awarded the 1921 Prize. Strangely enough, Einstein did not win the award for his special theory of relativity. Rather, he was given the award for his discovery of the law of the photoelectric effect. How was it possible that it took so long for one of the greatest scientists ever to receive the Nobel Prize? Why was he not given the award for his science-altering work on the special theory of relativity?

The simple explanation is that when Einstein first introduced his theory of relativity very few people understood it. It was a theory, not something proven experimentally, and members of the science community and the voting members on the Nobel committee were concerned about awarding a Prize for something not yet proven, no matter how astonishing or ground-breaking it was.

There was also the question as to whether the special theory of relativity satisfied the criteria set forth by Alfred Nobel for consideration of the Prize. Without quantifiable proof the theory could not be classified as a discovery, and it was not an invention. No matter how important the work, there was hesitation to acknowledge it by awarding the Nobel Prize.

Author Irving Wallace spent a great deal of time interviewing people while writing *The Prize*, his novel about the award. What he discovered in talking to people, including Nobel judge Dr. Sven Hedin, was that Einstein's ethnicity might have also played a part in his many rejections.

Einstein was Jewish. It did not matter that he had long before ceased to identify himself with any particular religion. Anti-Semitism (hostility or discrimination against Jews) was widespread throughout Europe, and the scientific

A photograph of Einstein in 1920, about one year before he was finally awarded the Nobel Prize in Physics.

community was not immune. German scientist Philipp Lenard, who himself won the Nobel Prize in Physics in 1905 for his work on cathode rays, was a vocal opponent of Einstein. Lenard dismissed the theory of relativity as "absurd," and campaigned against Einstein for almost a decade, telling the Nobel judges that relativity had "never been proved" and was "valueless."[1]

Lenard became a rabid Nazi Party supporter after Germany's defeat in World War I. He exercised great influence over the Nobel judges, including Dr. Hedin. Lenard's reputation was seriously tarnished when he became a supporter of Hitler's Nazi Party and attacked Einstein's "Jewish" physics. Hedin himself later became a Nazi sympathizer, who was pleased to count Nazi war criminals Hermann Göring, Heinrich Himmler, and Adolf Hitler as his close friends. Perhaps one can understand then—given the anti-Semitic rhetoric coming from colleagues like Lenard and the incomprehension over the relativity theory by the Nobel judges—why Einstein was rejected for the Nobel Prize so many times.

When Albert Einstein was finally named the winner of the 1921 Nobel Prize for Physics, he was its twentieth recipient. He joined an already prestigious list that included inventor Guglielmo Marconi, and physicists Max Planck, Marie Curie, and Wilhelm Röntgen. Röntgen won the very first Nobel Prize in Physics for his discovery of the X-ray. Some of the other early recipients were people Einstein came to know in the scientific community during the years he was establishing himself for his own theoretical work.

After having waited so long for the Nobel Prize, Einstein was not even in attendance when it was awarded.

A trip to Japan to deliver a series of lectures during this time had been planned since mid-September 1922. On October 8, in Marseilles, France, Einstein and his wife, Elsa, boarded the Japanese ship *Kitano Maru*, which was bound for Kobe, Japan. En route to their final destination, Albert and Elsa made stops in Singapore, Hong Kong, and Shanghai. On November 9, while Einstein was at sea somewhere between Hong Kong and Shanghai, he received a telegram informing him that the Swedish Academy of Sciences was awarding him the Nobel Prize "for his services to Theoretical Physics, and especially for his discovery of the law of the photoelectric effect."[2]

Even after his selection, Einstein could not escape controversy over the Nobel Prize. The question of Einstein's citizenship was raised because it is customary for a Nobel laureate to be accompanied to the award presentation by the diplomatic envoy of his or her country. If for some reason a laureate were unable to attend the ceremony, as was the case with Einstein, then the envoy would actually accept the award on his or her behalf. Einstein had at one time been a German citizen, but he now held Swiss citizenship, so the diplomatic representatives from both countries claimed the right to the honor. To resolve the problem gracefully, Swedish minister Sten Ramel presented Einstein his Nobel Prize scroll and medal in Berlin. Because of German currency restrictions, Einstein requested that the $32,000 prize money be transferred directly from Sweden to Switzerland.

On December 10, 1922, Professor S. Arrhenius, Chairman of the Nobel Committee for Physics of the Royal Swedish Academy of Sciences, delivered the presentation speech in Albert Einstein's absence. After addressing the guests in attendance, Arrhenius began his speech giving Einstein recognition for his work on his theory of relativity:

> There is probably no physicist living today whose name has become so widely known as that of Albert Einstein. Most discussion centers on his theory of relativity. This pertains essentially to epistemology and has therefore been the subject of lively debate in philosophical circles. It will be no secret that the famous philosopher Bergson in Paris has challenged this theory, while other philosophers have acclaimed it wholeheartedly. The theory in question also has astrophysical implications which are being rigorously examined at the present time.[3]

Arrhenius went on to explain Einstein's studies on liquids with solid particles suspended in them. He then discussed Einstein's role in the further development of quantum theory, particularly the law of the photoelectric effect, for which he was receiving the Nobel Prize.

Einstein explained the photoelectric effect within the context of quantum physics. The photoelectric effect can be defined as a process whereby light falling on a surface knocks electrons (particles that have a negative charge of electricity and travel around the nucleus of an atom) out of the surface. First, one had to accept that light behaved like a stream of particles, which were called photons. Each electron is ejected by a single photon or light quantum striking the surface. In quantum theory, the frequency, f, of the light determines the energy, E, of the photons in that light beam.

Einstein's own explanation of this effect was that a light quantum "penetrates like a minute missile into a metal, there encounters an electron, and transfers its whole energy to that electron."[4]

To fulfill his laureate obligations, Einstein later presented a lecture to an audience of 2,000 that included the Swedish king during the Scandinavian Scientists' Convention in Götenborg. Although it was customary for a laureate to give a lecture on the subject for which he had received his award, Einstein gave his on the *Fundamental Ideas and Problems of the Theory of Relativity*. What is even more interesting about that day is that Einstein, despite gaining international attention for his theory of relativity, would have preferred to give a lecture on a new theory he was developing—"the essential unity of gravity and electromagnetism."

One aspect of Albert Einstein was consistent: He was never satisfied with what he had already established—like a tumbleweed he was always on the move, searching for new questions and new discoveries.

An Unremarkable Youth

Albert Einstein was born in Ulm, Wurttemberg, Germany on March 14, 1879. Ulm was a town with plenty of old-time character situated alongside the Danube River. Its narrow, winding streets are typical of the kind pictured on postcards and paintings from the nineteenth century. Located in the hilly region at the base of the Swabian Alps, Ulm was most noteworthy for its great cathedral that claimed to have the tallest spire in Europe.

Einstein's father, Hermann, came from Buchau, a farm village on Lake Federnsee about 30 miles south of Ulm. From about 1577, Jews had settled in the area and established a thriving community. Despite the increase of anti-Semitism over the centuries, the Jews remained, even beyond the burning of the Buchau synagogue in 1938. The last Jew on record there was Siegbert Einstein, who died in

1968. Siegbert was a distant relative of the man who would later be named the Man of the Twentieth Century.

According to records kept by the Jewish authorities, the Einstein family had lived in Buchau since the mid-1700s. Albert's great-grandfather was born in Buchau in 1759, as was his grandfather, Abraham (1808), and his father, Hermann (1847). Abraham Einstein was a merchant by trade and was able to make a comfortable living to care for his family. Young Hermann was sent to Stuttgart (the capital of Wurttemburg) to enroll in high school, where he showed some aptitude for mathematics. When Hermann was nineteen, the Einsteins moved to Ulm.

It was after moving to Ulm that Hermann met Pauline Koch, who lived in the nearby town of Cannstadt. The Koch family was also Swabian, having settled in Jebenhausen, a northern region of the Alps. Pauline's father, Julius, ran a small bakery before moving the family to Cannstadt, just outside Stuttgart, in 1852. Once settled, Julius and his brother, Heinrich, began running a grain business that became rather lucrative in just a few years, making both brothers very wealthy. Julius's daughter, Pauline, enjoyed a privileged upbringing. She received a well-rounded education and had a bit of talent in music.

Although Pauline was eleven years younger than Hermann, they settled into a comfortable courtship and married in 1876. For the first year of their marriage, the Einsteins lived in Buchau. In 1877, they moved back to Ulm, the town whose residents proclaimed "Ulmense sunt mathematici" (the people of Ulm are mathematicians). In 1879, with Pauline already six months pregnant with her first child, the Einsteins moved into an apartment at No. 135,

20 Bahnhofstrasse. Their new home was convenient for Hermann, because it was just a few hundred yards away from the electrical and engineering business he had established with the financial help of Pauline's parents.

On March 14, 1879, Pauline gave birth to a son whom they named Albert. Upon seeing the child for the first time, members of both sides of the family were concerned. Apparently, newborn Albert was a rather large baby. His grandmother as much as said that he was too fat. Pauline thought her son's head was too large and had an angular shape. Doctors assured the Einsteins that there was nothing abnormal about their son and that in time he would look more normal.

Pauline and Hermann showered their son with love and affection. Still, they were concerned. Albert was a quiet baby and seemed developmentally slow. Some biographical accounts of his early years contend that Albert did not speak until he was almost three years of age. From his own recollections, Einstein affirmed this fact. He explained his lateness of speech as something he consciously chose to do, forgoing baby talk for a time until he could speak in fluent sentences. However, his maternal grandmother, Jette, wrote after a visit with her grandson when he was only two years old, saying, "He was so good and dear and we talk again and again of his droll ideas."[1]

Whatever the case, Einstein was apparently slow to speak and then later measured his thoughts before expressing himself. There are those who have even suggested that Einstein, like so many other great minds in history including Leonardo da Vinci, Michelangelo, Thomas Edison, and Alexander Graham Bell, suffered from a form of dyslexia, a disability in which the individual has difficulties making the basic connection between symbols (letters) and their sounds. Dyslexics often experience difficulties with concentration and verbal skills, receive poor grades, and are seen as underachievers. Although the cause or causes for his developmental slowness as a toddler remain unclear, even Einstein's teachers did not think there was much promise in his future.

Albert was less than a year old when his father's business failed. The collapse of the business didn't ruffle Hermann; he merely moved on to the next prospect. Relocating the family to the more cosmopolitan city of Munich in 1880, Hermann opened a modest electrochemical works with his brother, Jakob. The youngest of the Einstein children, Jakob was the only one of the five brothers to have a higher education. He became an engineer and settled in Munich after the Franco-Prussian War of 1870, where he managed a small company that handled water and gas installations.

Hermann, Pauline, and Albert moved into a small home they shared with Jakob just outside the heart of Munich. The partners named their company Jakob Einstein & Cie, with each brother working in his areas of expertise. Jakob handled the technical aspects of the business, while Hermann managed the commercial concerns.

The capital city of Bavaria was much different from the rural town of Ulm. Munich had a population of close to 250,000 people, 84 percent of whom were Catholic. Numerous churches like St. Mariahilf and the Jesuit St. Michael's dotted the city streets. The air was often filled with the ringing sound of church tower bells. Munich, a bustling city on the river Isar, had narrow winding streets and splendid architecture, as well as some of the finest art galleries in Europe.

The Einsteins really did not fit the obvious culture or history of Munich. Catholicism was the predominant religion, although there were Jewish families. Some practiced their religion; some assimilated (were absorbed into the German culture); and some Jewish families like the Einsteins were not particularly religious. One thing the Einsteins shared with their religious ancestry, however, was a deep respect for learning and a driving thirst for knowledge. Years later, Einstein was to become one of several European-born Jews to play a crucial role in many of the pioneering developments in the physical sciences, including Paul Ehrenfest (quantum theory), Lise Meitner (nuclear fission), and Leo Szilard (nuclear chain reaction).

In most ways the Einsteins were only Jewish by birth, not in faith. They did not attend synagogue, nor did they obey certain dietary laws like eating meat and dairy together or buying only kosher meat (animals slaughtered in accordance with Jewish law). As a result, Albert Einstein was raised in an environment that had broken with its Jewish traditions, reared instead in a family seeking independence and freedom from religious authority. Because the Einsteins were not practicing Jews, Albert had little trouble adjusting to his Catholic surroundings.

Just shy of his third birthday, Albert became the big brother of a baby sister, Maja, born on November 18, 1881. In preparing him for the baby's arrival, Pauline and Hermann told Albert that he would have a new playmate. Albert must have been expecting a toy, because upon seeing Maja he is reported to have said, "Where are the wheels?"

Only slightly more than two years younger than her brother, Maja would come to be one of Albert's closest companions and confidants throughout the rest of her life.

From her own biographical notes it is known that, as a youngster, Albert was pretty much a loner, preferring to shape his building blocks into enormous structures or taking on the challenge of constructing large houses of card formations and solving intricate puzzles rather than playing in the yard with neighboring kids or visiting cousins. Even as a child Einstein preferred the role of observer rather than participant when he found himself with other children.

Although outsiders thought of Albert as a quiet, withdrawn little fellow, his parents and sister knew another side of him, as well—he was also known to have a bit of a temper. On one occasion, while being tutored in his studies at home, Albert threw a chair at the teacher. Maja often found herself the recipient of Albert's tantrums, too, recounting in her memoirs how one time Albert struck her in the head with a pickax. Fortunately, Albert outgrew these fits of rage by the time he started school.

Albert had his first brush with the wonders of science when he was about five years old, while sick in bed. To cheer his son up a bit, his father brought him an unusual gift: a magnetic compass. Albert had never seen such a device before. He shook and twisted the compass every which way, but the needle always pointed north. He was intrigued by the device, and puzzled by how it worked. Years later Einstein wrote of the experience, "I can still remember—or at least believe I can remember—that this experience made a deep and lasting impression on me. Something deeply hidden had to be behind things."[2] This, perhaps, was the moment Albert Einstein began cultivating his quest to uncover the mysteries of the universe.

Although not easily engaged in activities, Albert had two parents who saw to it that their children were exposed to the arts, particularly literature and music. Hermann often read poetry to Albert and Maja in the evenings after dinner. He read from writers including Johann Christop Friedrich von Schiller, considered the founder of modern German literature. Among Schiller's works are *Mary Stuart*, *William Tell*, and the lyric poem *Ode to Joy*. Hermann also recited poetry, including poems by Heinrich Heine, a German Jew whose lyric poetry includes *Die Lorelei*, the tale of the legendary siren whose beauty and alluring songs beckoned sailors into the dangerous narrows of the Rhine River, where the rock reefs and waves devoured them.

Pauline Einstein's love was music. An accomplished pianist in her own right, Pauline wanted her children to develop an appreciation for music. Wanting Albert to learn a musical instrument, Pauline chose the violin. At his first lesson at the age of six, Albert had one of his tantrums. Albert's outburst did not discourage his mother. She simply hired another teacher. Albert wound up continuing with his violin lessons until he was thirteen. Despite discontinuing his formal training, Albert derived a great deal of pleasure from playing the violin, often playing with other musicians as a young man. Playing the violin was one of Albert's joys, and remained so throughout his life.

Until he became a teen, Albert had not liked the repetition and drills of practicing a musical instrument. In fact, Albert found the whole issue of learning by rote (repeating something without much thought) distasteful—whether it was music, history, or any other subject. Ultimately, if he became interested in certain musical pieces, he worked on learning them on his own. Of the revelation, Einstein said:

> I only began to learn something after I was thirteen, when I had fallen in love mainly with Mozart's sonatas. My wish to reproduce them to some degree in their artistic content and their unique gracefulness forced me to improve my technique; this I acquired with those sonatas, without ever practicing systematically. I believe altogether that love is a better teacher than a sense of duty—at least for me.[3]

Einstein carried his dislike for having to learn information mechanically into his school years. In fact, there was a lot about attending school that Albert did not like. When he turned six, he began attending the Petersschule on Blumenstrasse, a Catholic elementary school within walking distance from the Einstein home. Because the Einsteins were not particularly religious, and the only Jewish private school in Munich had closed its doors due to a lack of students seven years before Albert's birth, Petersschule on Blumenstrasse would suffice.

Einstein was the only Jew in a class of seventy students. Munich was a rather progressive city for the times, so the teachers were rather liberal and did not openly single out non-Catholics. Albert did not experience any overt discrimination, but again found himself clearly an outsider. Einstein recalled his treatment, saying:

> Among the children at the elementary school anti-Semitism was prevalent. It was based on racial characteristics of which the children were strangely aware and on impressions from religious teaching. Physical

Albert Einstein and his younger sister, Maja, as children.

> attacks and insults on the way home from school were frequent, but for the most part not too vicious. But they were sufficient to consolidate even in a child a lively sense of being an outsider.[4]

Although the Einstein family was not particularly religious, there was a brief period when young Albert embraced religion. In his quest to learn, Albert wanted to know how God created the world. Yet after reading several passages in the Bible, Albert came to feel that much of the stories relayed in the Bible could not be true. Faith had to be replaced by quantifiable information.

As he had at home, Albert spoke slowly, choosing his words carefully before answering a question posed to him in class by his teacher. He did not do particularly well in his studies and his teachers thought he was rather unintelligent. Albert did not like the strict environment or the rote method of teaching. Biographer Philipp Frank explained, "The students were required to learn mechanically and the main emphasis was placed on . . . obedience and discipline. The pupils were required to stand at attention when addressed by the teacher and were not supposed to speak unless asked a question."[5]

When Albert turned nine, he transferred to the Luitpold Gymnasium (European countries often call schools before university-level education gymnasiums), a school that was even more strict and rigid than his elementary school. Years later, an adult Einstein would say that his teachers in elementary school were like sergeants and the ones at the gymnasium were like lieutenants. Again, most subjects did not interest him, but he did enjoy reading the literature assigned, which included Schiller, Johann Wolfgang von

Goethe, and the English dramatist William Shakespeare. Still, his teachers were sure he would not amount to much.

He was subjected to admonishments from his teachers in many scholastic areas, but Albert did show an aptitude for Latin and mathematics. He especially liked math because it was logical. Albert had gotten his introduction to math at home. In fact, it was at home that twelve-year-old Einstein began to get the intellectual stimulation to spark his interest. There were two men who were responsible for motivating Albert to learn—his uncle, Jakob, and Max Talmey, a frequent house-guest. Uncle Jakob introduced his nephew to algebra (mathematics used to find an unknown number) while the young Einstein was still in grade school. Jakob engaged Albert's interest in algebra by explaining it as "a merry science in which we go hunting for a little animal whose name we don't know. So we call it X. When we bag the game we give it the right name."[6]

"Something deeply hidden had to be behind things."

—Albert Einstein

Albert relished the lunch visits when Jakob would come and give him complex math problems to solve. He was exposed to a new wonder of science when he received a little book on Euclidean geometry (a branch of mathematics that deals with points, lines, angles, surfaces, and solids). These axioms had been accepted for more than two thousand years, so applying Euclidean geometry to concrete objects was a natural progression for scientists and mathematicians. When Einstein discovered the wonders of geometry, he thought it was terrific that man could achieve "such a level of certainty and purity in thought, as the Greeks first demonstrated in geometry."[7]

Albert's other unofficial teacher, Max Talmey, was a regular Thursday guest at the Einstein home. Practicing the European Jewish custom of inviting a poor student to lunch, the Einsteins opened their home to Talmey, a medical student who had little means to support himself. Eleven years older than Albert, Talmey saw the boy's interest in learning about science and math and often brought books for him to read, including *Force and Matter* by Ludwig Buchner, *Popular Books of Physical Science* by Aaron Bernstein, and *Kosmos* by Alexander von Humboldt. Albert consumed the information in the books and often discussed what he read with Talmey during his weekly lunch engagements.

Albert's gift of genius was beginning to show. It was not long before he was studying higher mathematics on his own and had forged ahead of Talmey's own knowledge on the subject. So Talmey next introduced Albert to philosophy, loaning him books to read including Immanuel Kant's *A Critique of Pure Reason*. Kant's works are often difficult for college students to comprehend, but his ideas did not seem to be a problem for Albert to understand. Kant had suggested some bizarre ideas in his writings, like stating that the planets in our universe had been or will be inhabited or that time and space are not really the results of experience but rather a figment of our own imagination. Kant postulated that the way to end world wars was to establish a "world" government. He even dared to suggest that God really did not exist.

Judging by his performance in school, Albert was not going to be a stellar student. He continued his unhappy existence at the gymnasium into his fifteenth birthday, when things suddenly changed. Hermann and Jakob's business was failing in Munich. With the financial help of the Koch family in Genoa, Italy, the brothers decided to open a new electrical business in the Italian city of Milan. That decision meant that Hermann had to move the family from Germany to Italy. However, Albert's parents decided it was best for him to remain in Munich and finish his high school education. In June of 1894, Hermann sold the house and he, Pauline, Maja, and Uncle Jakob left for Milan. Albert was sent to live at a boarding house until he earned his diploma from the gymnasium.

Albert was immediately struck by how lonely it was at the boarding house. He knew no one, and his only visitor was a distant relative who came by occasionally to check on him. Albert grew depressed. He knew that he needed the diploma if he wanted to study at a university. He also knew that if he remained in Germany, he would have to serve in the military by age sixteen.

Going to school became an abysmal chore, and Albert wanted more and more to leave Munich and join his family in Italy. With his depression deepening, Albert sought the help of the family doctor. Seeing how anxious he was, the doctor wrote a note to the gymnasium administrators explaining that Einstein could have a nervous breakdown if he was not permitted to convalesce with the rest of his family. Einstein's math teacher gave a further boost to his cause by agreeing that there was nothing more that he could teach him at Luitpold. The gymnasium administration was almost relieved to give the troubled student permission to withdraw. Given his freedom, Albert left Munich and hoped life would be better in Italy.

CHAPTER THREE

SWITZERLAND: AN OASIS IN EUROPE

Much to the surprise and dismay of his parents, Albert arrived in Milan shortly before Christmas recess. Even though he was now a high school dropout with no definite plans for the future, Albert was elated to be free of the "lieutenants" and mandatory German military service looming over him. He may have been happy to be back with his family, but his timing was not the best. Hermann's new business venture was struggling and he felt burdened by his dropout son's arrival. Still, his sister Maja recalled that she sensed that her brother's spirits lifted once he was out of Germany and reunited with his family. He was no longer the outcast dreamer who stayed mostly to himself. He was more outgoing and social in Milan than she ever remembered him being in Munich.

Albert tried to reassure his disappointed parents that he

fully intended to complete his education and get his diploma. Jakob suggested that Albert attend the Swiss Federal Institute of Technology in Zurich (also known in Swiss German as Eidgenössische Technische Hochschule, or ETH), a university in Switzerland with a first-rate international reputation. If he passed the entrance exam, he would not even have to take the time to finish high school first. Albert proposed to study all summer in preparation for taking the exam in the fall. He also helped out where he could with the family's failing business when he was not studying, working through calculations to solve technical problems that stymied his uncle.

With the hope of expanding the business and being awarded the contract to set up a hydroelectric plant in the town of Pavia, the Einsteins moved there in the spring of 1895. Albert later wrote to a friend in Switzerland that the city was drab and dirty, its only bright spot being their "delightful, graceful little children."[1] However, Italy's aura—its landscape, language, people, and culture—left an enduring impression on Albert. Years later, during correspondence with mathematician Tullio Levi-Civita, Albert asked his colleague to write back to him in Italian saying, "You can hardly imagine the pleasure it gives me to receive such a genuine Italian letter. It revives in me the most beautiful memories of my youth."[2]

During this summer, Albert also wrote his first "physical" essay. Entitled *über die Untersuchung des Aetherzustandes im magnetischen Feld* (Examination of the State of the Ether in the Magnetic Field), the essay discusses the "theory" that electricity, magnetism, and the ether (a mysterious element that was believed to fill all space and the means by which electromagnetic waves transmit themselves) were somehow connected. He sent the essay to his favorite uncle, Caesar Koch. Needless to say, it was with great pride that Uncle Caesar displayed his nephew's paper.

As the summer came to a close, Albert traveled by railcar to Zurich to stay with former Ulm resident and family friend, Gustav Maier. A timid Albert reported for the ETH entrance exam on October 8, 1895. It was not an easy test even for the brightest examinees, taking place over several days and covering many different subjects. Despite occasional displays of astonishing intellect, Albert failed the exam. Recalling how he felt, Albert said that "it made me realize painfully the gappy character of my previous schooling, even though the examiners were patient and understanding."[3]

Although an unexpected and traumatic blow to Albert, it was not a total setback. He had scored so high in the math and science sections that the examiners recognized his potential. Principal Albin Herzog, acknowledging that Albert (age sixteen) was two years younger than most of the students who took the exam, promised to admit Albert the following year as long as he acquired a high school diploma.

In order to earn his diploma, Albert enrolled at the province school in Aarau, a Swiss town near Zurich and the German border. Initially Albert was a little apprehensive about going to northern Switzerland, close to the German border. Many of the people who lived in that area were of German origin. He worried that he would end up right back amid the rigid, strict educational environment he had left behind in Munich. However, as the train got closer to

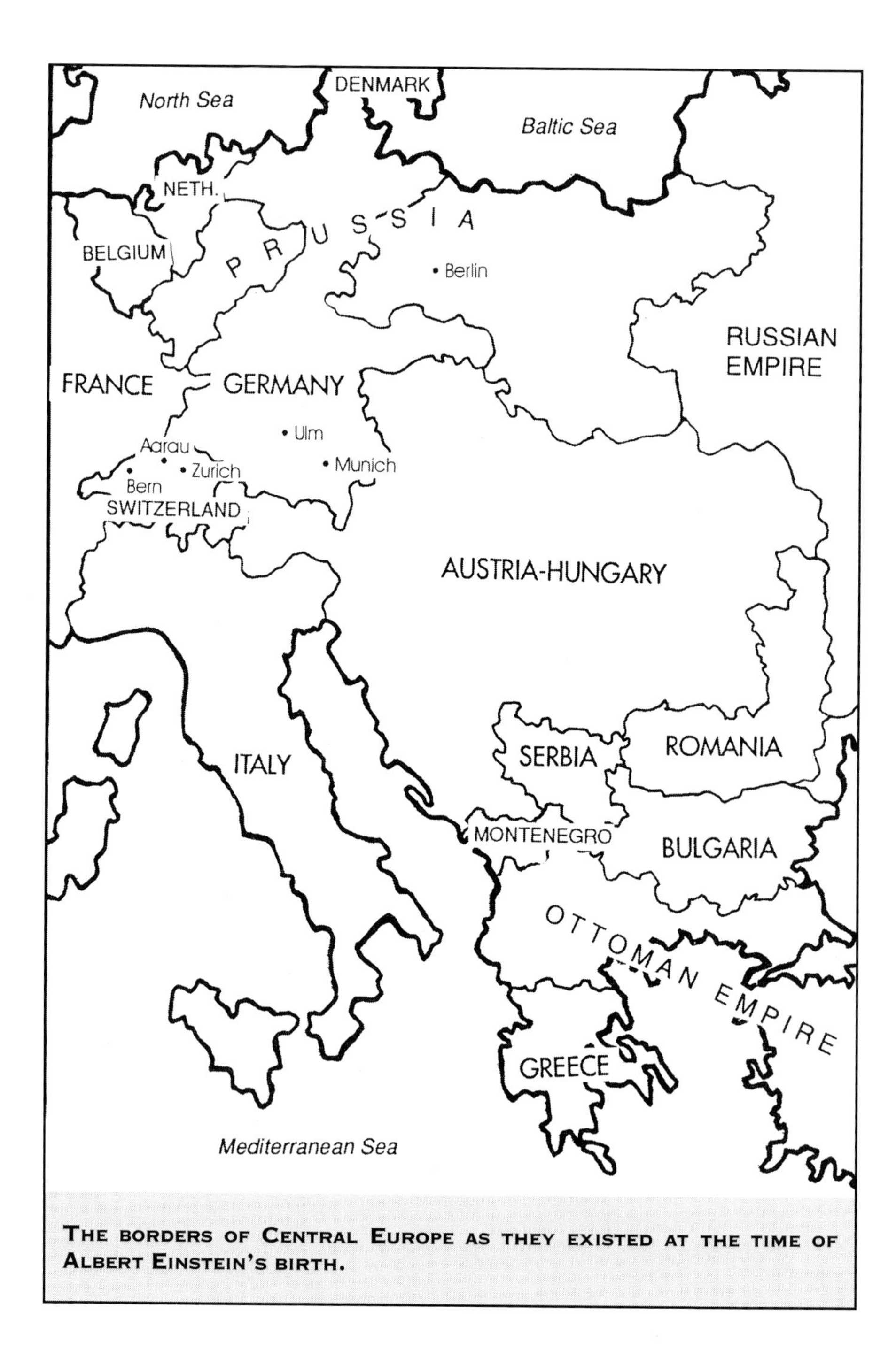

The borders of Central Europe as they existed at the time of Albert Einstein's birth.

Aarau, his fears eased as he rode through the beautiful Swiss countryside. He later described Aarau as "an unforgettable oasis in that European oasis, Switzerland."[4]

Albert came to embrace his time in Aarau, and he stopped dreading the experience ahead. One of the school's appeals, besides its terrific academic reputation, was that Albert would not have to endure living in another boardinghouse. Again providing assistance for Albert, Maier arranged for him to stay with one of the school's teachers, Jost Winteler. Winteler agreed to take Albert into his home as a paying lodger. Although Winteler and his wife, Pauline, already had a rather large family (four sons and three daughters), Albert was assured of having his own room, thereby guaranteeing him some privacy.

Two significant events occurred during Albert's time in Aarau. The first had to do with his host family. The Wintelers not only provided Albert with a comfortable place to stay, but they became like a second family to the teen while away from his own home. Such a close bond was established that Albert remained friends with the Wintelers throughout his life. In fact, there was to be a permanent family connection—Albert's sister, Maja, eventually married the Wintelers' son, Paul; later his close friend from ETH, Michele Besso, married the Wintelers' eldest daughter, Anna.

Albert himself experienced his first romance with another of the Wintelers' daughters, eighteen-year-old Marie. Albert was two years younger than Marie, but he became smitten with her while staying at the Winteler residence. She had just completed teacher training at a local college, but was still living at home when Albert arrived.

Much to Albert's delight, the Winteler household had a relaxed atmosphere. Jost, who taught history and classical literature, encouraged lively conversation amongst household members and guests on just about any topic.

Occasionally Jost would take a few of the older children and some of his students out on bird-watching expeditions on the weekends. Albert and Marie often went along, more to share time alone together than to spot a rare bird in the countryside. Marie, like Albert, was musically trained and often joined Albert in duets by playing piano to his violin. By now Albert was very "attached" to his violin and played it whenever time permitted. However, judging by his grades, it appeared that he was perhaps spending too much time on bird-watching excursions and impromptu recitals. As usual, his grades in math and physics were great, but those in French language and subjects he was not interested in were poor.

Soon the relationship between Albert and Marie turned romantic. Both the Wintelers and the Einsteins were aware of the budding relationship between their children. At home during Easter break visiting with his family in Pavia, Albert wrote to Marie, who he now called his "beloved darling." In his letters he wrote how vital she was to his own happiness, telling her, "You mean more to my soul than the whole world did before."[5] For the moment, it seemed that Albert's heart belonged to Marie.

The other significant event in Albert's life during his year in Aarau had to do with his internal struggle over his citizenship. There is no way to identify with certainty when Albert no longer wished to be a German, but records show that he was officially granted release of his citizenship on

January 28, 1896, "for the purpose of his emigration to Italy."[6] Whether it was to avoid conscription into the military or his general discomfort with the German way of life, he became stateless six weeks before his seventeenth birthday. He needed little reassurance for his decision, as he often heard "papa" Winteler speak about the potential threat of Imperial German expansionism. Because of his intense respect and affection for Swiss native/mentor Jost Winteler, Albert had no reservations about deciding to apply for Swiss citizenship.

Upon graduating from Aarau with the required diploma, Albert was able to begin his college studies at ETH. During his final exams, Einstein had written a paper for his French class outlining his objectives for the Polytechnic, including his career goal. "My idea is to become a teacher in these fields of natural science and I will choose the theoretical part of these sciences."[7] Einstein believed that his talents lay in the natural sciences, and also liked the idea that the profession afforded a great deal of independence.

The Polytechnic Institute was founded in 1855. It was the first university-type school of the Swiss Confederation, and therefore was overseen by the Swiss government in Bern. Gottfried Semper, the institute's first professor of architecture, designed the ETH's main building. Considered one of the most stunning structures in the city, it offered a beautiful view of Zurich's historic center city. The Polytechnic was small, with a population of less than a thousand students at the turn of the twentieth century.

In mid-October 1896, Einstein enrolled in Division VI A, which was the "School for Specialized Teachers in the

Mathematical and Science Subjects."[8] Division VI A at the ETH was for math and physics teachers who wanted to teach at the secondary level. If one wished to teach at a university level, it was necessary to acquire a doctorate elsewhere. Eventually, Einstein did just that when he began applying for research assistantships. Aside from providing mathematical and scientific instruction for engineers, Division VI A was also mindful of the need for vital research in the fields of science including math, physics, and astronomy.

Einstein's life changed upon enrolling at the Polytechnic. It changed for Marie, too, who moved out of the Winteler home after securing a first-grade teaching job at a school in another town. She and Einstein continued to write regularly for a while before Einstein's letters stopped. His attentions had shifted to another woman, Mileva Maric, who was a classmate at the Institute. Maric was a rather quiet student who came from Serbia. She was the only female student majoring in physics along with Einstein at ETH, which was a rarity because not many women pursued higher educations in science. The ETH was also one of the few places in Europe where a woman was allowed to obtain a college degree.

Family and friends were puzzled by the interest the two showed in one another because they seemed so different. Although evidently bright enough to get into ETH, Maric was three years older than Einstein, and was often sullen and moody. She was not what men would call beautiful, and walked with a slight limp due to a defective hip. Women were drawn to Einstein because of his rather exotic appearance and his intelligence, and were enchanted by the melodious sounds of his violin playing. The best people could make of the relationship between Maric and Einstein was that they were both outsiders in a predominantly Swiss student population.

Still, Einstein and Maric enjoyed a pleasant enough environment in Zurich despite being "outsiders." Although not a traditional social student, not long after his arrival at ETH Einstein made the acquaintance of two gentlemen who would become lifelong friends—Marcel Grossmann and Michele Besso. Grossmann, a year older than Einstein, was a mathematics student at the Polytechnic. Once a week, the two young men would go to the Café Metropol and discuss and debate everything from math and physics to philosophy and the universe. Grossmann was also a lifesaver for his less than organized friend. He attended every lecture and kept meticulous notes. Grossmann gladly shared these notebooks of information with Einstein when it came time to prepare for exams. Einstein was grateful for his friend's unselfishness: "I would rather not speculate how I might have fared without them."[9]

Einstein met Michele Besso at the Zurich home of Selina Caprotti, a woman who opened her parlor every Saturday afternoon for people to come and play their music. Einstein often brought his violin and played duets with some of the women guests who played piano. Besso, six years Einstein's senior, was a native of Zurich, although he had grown up in Italy. He excelled in mathematics and studied mechanical engineering at the Polytechnic, graduating five years ahead of Einstein. The two found they shared among other things a mutual passion for engaging in thoughtful scientific discussions, and they became fast friends. It was Einstein who introduced Besso to Anna Winteler, whom he married in 1898.

Hoping to teach mathematical physics upon graduation from the ETH, Einstein had to devote his studies to both mathematics and the natural sciences. Under the guidance of six professors, including Hermann Minkowski, Heinrich Weber, Alfred Wolfer, and Jean Pernet, Einstein took courses in advanced geometry, calculus, astrophysics, and astronomy. He also took classes in subjects he enjoyed including philosophy and literature.

As a university student, Einstein continued to display the same independent and disdainful attitude toward his professors as he had his autocratic teachers in Munich. On one occasion as a third-year student, he infuriated Pernet after casually depositing the instructions on how to conduct an experiment in the laboratory into the trashcan without even bothering to look at it because he had decided to do it another way. During the experiment, he wound up injuring his hand so severely that he required stitches. Pernet complimented Einstein on his enthusiasm, but doubted his future success in the field of physics. "For your own good you should switch to something else, medicine maybe, literature, or law," Pernet told Einstein.[10]

Einstein greatly admired his math professor Hermann Minkowski, but the admiration was not reciprocated. Minkowski, who did not see the same enthusiasm from Einstein as his colleague had, thought he was lazy. Einstein also displeased physics professor Weber with his indifferent study habits and irritated him by calling him "Herr Weber" instead of the more deferential "Herr Professor." His tendency to exhibit this disregarding kind of attitude would later hinder Einstein when he tried to secure employment upon graduation.

Einstein had his own issues with Weber. He was disappointed that Weber did not include in his coverage of the history portion of physics any discussions of James Maxwell. Maxwell's mathematical equations eventually helped to explain many of the unknown aspects of electricity that led to the development of the radio, television, and radar. Einstein would cut classes and read Maxwell's theories. Exposure to Maxwell's work later became critical to Einstein's own theoretical work on the natural sciences.[11]

Even in his leisure time Einstein's mind was consumed with thoughts of physics, and he let himself contemplate the ideas of his contemporaries and those who came before him. Despite being so captivated by the realm of physics, Einstein did not deprive himself of other pleasures like watching a sunset on his porch while he puffed away on his pipe; reading works by his favorite poet, Heinrich Heine; or indulging in his newfound love of sailing on Lake Zurich.

Still, even while relaxing Einstein was always thinking about the physical world, about time and space and what exists within it, and how we perceive the world around us. He read books that delved into the works by Maxwell, as well as University of Berlin physics professor Hermann von Helmholtz and his colleague Gustav Kirchhoff. A versatile scholar, von Helmholtz devoted much of his time to exploration and research in such areas as physiology, chemistry, and magnetism. His work in examining the connection of matter to ether was of particular interest to Einstein.

Unfortunately, von Helmholtz died before he was able to test his theories.

Von Helmholtz's assistant, Heinrich Hertz, continued to explore the electromagnetic theories of Maxwell, and in one experiment was successful in producing radio waves. His experiment demonstrated that electromagnetic (radio) waves traveled at the same speed as light, and more importantly these waves, like light waves, could be reflected, altered or distorted, and polarized.

Because of Einstein's intense interest in how things behaved in time and space and in discovering the real nature of the universe, Michele Besso suggested that he read Ernst Mach's *Science of Mechanics*, which strongly criticized the idea of an absolute space and motion in the universe. Besso believed that Einstein was influenced by Mach's work when years later he was formulating his theory of relativity.

Early on in his studies, Einstein realized that he was more drawn to the natural sciences than to math because, as he explained in his autobiographical notes, "[I] saw that mathematics was split up into numerous specialties, each of which could easily absorb the short lifetime granted to us."[12] So it was physics that occupied most of Einstein's scholastic time. He loved being in the laboratory, where he delighted in what he called "direct contact with experience." He was fortunate that Grossmann, who recognized Einstein's potential, was happy to share his notes from math classes. Otherwise, Einstein might not have been so free to concentrate on the very work that would lead him to great discoveries later on.

During his fourth year at the Polytechnic, Einstein realized that he was still "stateless." He had submitted his

> *"[I] saw that mathematics was split up into numerous specialities, each of which could easily absorb the short lifetime granted to us."*
>
> **—Albert Einstein**

application and other required paperwork to apply for Swiss citizenship in October 1899. After much hullabaloo with permissions, questionnaires, investigations, and a police report, in March 1900 the Federal Council of the Swiss Confederation approved Einstein's application. His budding romance with Maric had by now become a serious relationship, and the two talked of marriage. But the most pressing issue for Einstein in the spring of 1900 was the approach of final exams and writing a required diploma essay. He and Maric submitted their essay ideas on heat conduction to Professor Weber, who approved them.

Their essays received adequate final grades of 4.5 (out of a top grade of 6) for Einstein and 4 for Maric. The subject course exams were another story. Five students assembled to take the final exams. Einstein and Maric, the two physics majors, did not fare as well as the three mathematics majors. Einstein received a final average of 4.91; Maric, a 4.0, which was the lowest numerical average among the five candidates. As a result, Maric was the only one who was not awarded a diploma. Einstein consoled Maric and assured her that she could take the exam the following year.

Surprisingly, Einstein had been traumatized by the pressure of preparing for the exam and thought it was one of the worst things he had endured in his life. He was grateful to have it behind him and looked toward finding employment and making wedding plans. Planning to spend his summer vacation with his family, Einstein returned to Italy filled with optimism about his future. Although Hermann and Pauline were happy that their son had graduated from the Polytechnic, they were concerned about him becoming gainfully employed. Hermann's latest business venture was floundering, and money was tight.

The conversation grew even graver when Einstein mentioned the prospect of marrying Maric. His parents were adamantly opposed. According to a letter Einstein wrote to Maric, his mother "buried her head in the pillows and wept like a child."[13] Pauline felt that her son would be ruining his future with a woman who was older. Perhaps another reason for the Einsteins' rather immediate disapproval of their son's relationship with Maric, although it was never explicitly stated, was the fact that she was not Jewish. Hermann also had a much more practical reason for opposing his son's wedding—how would he support himself and a wife without a job? Even though Einstein was sure he would be offered employment at the Polytechnic, he soon found out that securing *any* job would prove to be a difficult and daunting experience.

A Tenuous Start for an Improbable Genius

Einstein had been aware that his conduct and demeanor often irritated his professors while he was a student at the Zurich Polytechnic. Despite the fact that many of them, including Minkowski and Weber, communicated their annoyance with him, Einstein appeared unfazed by their displeasure. Also working against him was the fact that he did not demonstrate any extraordinary intellect, nor did he particularly stand out as an exceptional student. If Einstein had had those qualities, his professors might have been inclined to overlook his less than desirable attributes and embrace his presence in the student body.

Einstein assumed that finding a job would be a matter of course for him. Unfortunately, because of their negative view of Einstein, the faculty at the ETH showed no interest in offering him a paid position upon graduation. He felt humiliated when he found out that all his fellow graduates had been appointed research assistants at the Polytechnic. His outspokenness and sarcastic manner had alienated the very faculty members from whom he now sought employment. Even Alfred Stern, a history professor at the ETH with whom Einstein had forged a friendship, was unable to help him.

Realizing that he had to take a different path, Einstein began sending out queries for graduate research assistant positions to scientists in Germany. Foolishly, Einstein also used Weber's name as a reference. Although it is not clear that using Weber's name hurt Einstein's chances for employment, it definitely did not help him. Maric acknowledged to a friend that Einstein could be outspoken at times, but also speculated that there might be another issue at work, explaining, "My sweetheart has a very wicked tongue and is a Jew into the bargain."[1] Switzerland was probably less anti-Semitic than its border neighbor Germany, but bias against Jews was still not uncommon throughout most of Europe.

At the end of the family's vacation, Einstein agreed to spend some time with his father to learn the family business in case of an emergency. They traveled together for a few months before Einstein returned to Zurich and his beloved Maric. With money no longer coming from his wealthy aunt Julie Koch, Einstein and Maric earned occasional money from giving private tutoring.

While waiting for responses to his job queries, Einstein began working on his doctoral thesis. Inspired by the writings of Ludwig Boltzman on thermodynamics, Einstein wrote a paper on capillarity (the theory of liquids). It was within the study of what physicists called interface phenomena (the interaction of molecules and atoms) that Einstein thought he might come upon some new discoveries. He submitted the paper to *Annalen der Physik* (Annals of Physics), a well-respected German scholarly journal in December 1900. The editors accepted the paper for publication and informed Einstein that it would appear in their March 1901 issue.

Aware that his employment opportunities were dwindling, and armed with reprints of his article to mail with résumés, Einstein expanded his job search. He wrote to Wilhelm Ostwald (who went on to win the Nobel Prize in Chemistry in 1909), professor of physical chemistry at Leipzig University, inquiring about his need for a mathematical physicist. Although Einstein never received a reply, Ostwald would later submit Einstein's name for the Nobel Prize in 1910, 1912, and 1913. Einstein tried to land a job with another future Nobel laureate, Dutch physicist Heike Kamerlingh Onnes, also without success.

Without a job, the final approval for granting Einstein Swiss citizenship by the Great Municipal Council was in question. With no prospects and no money of his own, Einstein might become a burden to the state. However, in early 1901, the Council members agreed to meet young Einstein and question him on a variety of topics. Despite having read about a naïve, absent-minded physics student, the Council came away from their meeting with an entirely different perception of Einstein. On February 21, 1901, Einstein was awarded Swiss citizenship.[2]

With his citizenship settled, Einstein finally had one worry behind him. At one point he was so broke that he had to move back to Milan. Although discouraged about his situation and frustrated over his parents' continual badgering about his marriage plans, his mood brightened when he received a visit from friend Michele Besso. By now Besso had married Anna Winteler and was also a father. The two talked endlessly about physics—from the separation of matter from ether to how heat affected gases.

During this time, Einstein also received an unexpected lift from another Polytechnic friend, Marcel Grossmann. Grossmann had written Einstein a letter telling him that he had secured a permanent position at the Swiss Patent Office in Bern. It seemed that Grossmann's father was a friend of Friedrich Haller, the Patent Office director. Aware of Einstein's unemployment, Grossmann's father also recommended Einstein for the next available opening in the Patent Office. Marcel could not tell his colleague when the post would open, but Einstein was heartened by the prospect. He thanked Grossmann profusely, writing, "I am truly touched by your loyalty and humanity which did not let you forget your old luck-less friend. . . . Indeed hardly tell you that I would be happy to be granted such a fine field of activity, and that I would do everything in my power not to disgrace your recommendation."[3]

While awaiting the vacancy at the Patent Office, Einstein was blessed by more good news—he was offered a temporary teaching position at the Technical College in Winterthur. He would be filling in for math professor Adolf Gasser, who was being called away for military duty. Einstein had not applied for the job, but was grateful for the offer. The assignment would run from mid-May to mid-July. The weekend before he was to start his temporary job, Einstein took the train from Milan to Lake Como, Italy, to spend the time with Maric, who had traveled from Zurich to meet him. The two behaved like honeymooners, strolling through the wonderful gardens at the Villa Carlotta, and taking a horse-drawn sleigh ride up to the Alps.

Certain that things were getting better, Einstein left Maric and headed for Winterthur more relaxed than he had been in months. Despite a workload that included teaching six classes, Einstein found that he enjoyed teaching mathematics. Winterthur was also close to his sweetheart, so by taking the seventeen-mile train ride to Zurich, he was able to see Maric on the weekends. The most pleasant surprise for Einstein in his temporary assignment was that he found he was able to work full-time without being exhausted: "Having taught 5 or 6 hours in the morning, I am still quite fresh and work on my further education at the library in the afternoon, or on interesting problems at home."[4]

At some point during the latter part of May, Maric told Einstein that she was pregnant. Einstein seemed to take the news in stride. In a letter to Maric shortly after her news, he wrote "How's the boy,?"[5] reassuring Maric that everything was fine. He went on to write, "Be happy and don't fret, darling. I won't leave you and will bring everything to a happy conclusion. You just have to be patient! You'll see that my arms aren't so bad to rest in, even if things are beginning a little awkwardly."[6]

Maric's pregnancy could not have come at a worse time. Despite the obvious—she and Einstein were not yet married—her pregnancy would only alienate Einstein's parents further.

Hermann's business had just collapsed and he wanted his son to assume some of the financial support for his sister, Maja. Perhaps the most critical concern was that Einstein's job, and therefore his livelihood, would come to an end by mid-summer.

Einstein handled the pressure by throwing himself more intensely into his physics research and his teaching. When the post was up, he returned to Milan to spend the summer with his parents. He continued written correspondence with Maric in Zurich, never wavering in his assurances to her that everything would work out. Maric shared her disappointment with Einstein over the news that she had failed her ETH exams again. Although any thoughts of a teaching career now seemed out of the question for her, Einstein tried to encourage Maric by reminding her that they could always work as a team in scientific research. With the exam behind her and Einstein's reassuring words, Maric shifted her focus to thoughts of marriage and the birth of their child.

Einstein was not out of work for long after his temporary post at the Technical College ended. In September, he secured a tutoring job at a school in Schaffhausen, a Swiss town near the German border. The salary was not really adequate for a man who wanted to get married and was an expectant father, but it gave Einstein another reprieve from having to take an office job that was sure to make him miserable. The move sent Einstein farther away from Maric, however. By November, in her seventh month of pregnancy, Maric went to stay with her parents in Novi Sad, Serbia, until the baby was born.

Almost from the beginning of his new job, Einstein did

not really get along with his new boss. To balance his paltry salary (about $30 a month) Einstein was given free room and board at the home of the school's owner, Dr. Jakob Nuesch. Einstein did not like Dr. Nuesch. He felt he was overcharging his students, underpaying him, and pocketing a tidy profit. Influenced by unyielding discipline and the strict German rote method of teaching, Dr. Nuesch was not too happy with Einstein's easygoing style and unwillingness to force his students to give in to authority. The two had many heated arguments. Einstein tried to bide his time, waiting for the Patent Office job to be advertised.

Trying to keep busy during this dismal time, Einstein finished his doctoral dissertation on his theory of attraction forces between atoms in December 1901, and submitted it to Professor Alfred Kleiner at the University of Zurich. Einstein and Maric continued to write to each other. They even began to think that the baby might be a girl, and in their correspondence referred to her as "Lieserl."

During this time Einstein also heard from his friend Grossmann in Bern, who informed him that the Patent Office post would be advertised within days. Heartened, Einstein made a formal application for the vacancy: "I, the undersigned, herewith offer myself for the post of engineer Class II at the Federal Patent Office which is announced in the Bundesblatt of 11 December, 1901."[7] He went on to outline his education and training at the Polytechnic, and included his two jobs at Winterthur and Schaffhausen. He concluded the letter by adding that he had recently been granted his Swiss citizenship. Hopeful that everything would soon fall into place, Einstein remained in Schaffhausen over the Christmas holiday. He spent part of the time with Maja, who had come from Aarau to see her brother.

At the start of 1902, Einstein resumed his teaching at Schaffhausen. However, his adversarial relationship with Dr. Nuesch worsened. Claiming that he sensed the underlying rumbles of a revolutionary within Einstein, Nuesch finally fired him. He did not want any upheaval in his institution. Very little is known about what went on in Einstein's life during the month of January. However, one thing is certain: Faced with no job again and very little money, there was no longer any reason for Einstein to stay in Schaffhausen.

Perhaps hoping that the Patent Office job would come through, Einstein returned to Bern. Shortly after his arrival, he received a letter from Maric's father that had been forwarded from Schaffhausen—he was the father of a baby girl. Despite being "frightened out of his wits,"[8] Einstein joyously responded in a letter of his own asking questions like, "Is she healthy and does she cry properly? What are her eyes like? Which one of us does she more resemble?"[9] He asked Maric to send him a picture or drawing once she was able. How complicated the birth was remains unclear, but Maric's father did tell Einstein that Mileva was too weak to write to him herself.

Although Einstein wrote that he loved Lieserl—even though he had not yet seen his newborn daughter—it is doubtful that he ever did see her. After the letter from Maric's father, there is little mention of Lieserl in later letters between Einstein and Maric. Lieserl remained in Novi Sad with Maric and her parents, and there is speculation that she was later adopted, perhaps by relatives. Aside from his questions about his daughter, Einstein wrote Maric about the city of Bern and his interim plans. Although he described his apartment as large and beautiful, it was small and sparsely furnished. To support himself until he began at the Patent Office (a position he was almost certain he would get), he advertised lessons in mathematics and physics in the *Berner Anzeiger* (a Bern newspaper).

The first person to respond to the ad was a young Romanian student named Maurice Solovine. Although Einstein was offering lessons in math and science, Solovine thirsted for more in-depth examination of the philosophical fundamentals of physics. Soon the two were engaging in a deep conversation, attempting to decipher some of the mystifying secrets of the universe. Pupil and teacher continued to meet often, eventually developing a friendship that would last a lifetime.

By the summer, Einstein and Solovine were joined in their discussions by Conrad Habicht. Habicht was a fellow ETH graduate and was the one who had recommended Einstein for the job in Schaffhausen. For a fee of two francs each, hardly enough money even to pay for his pipe tobacco, Solovine and Habicht studied with Einstein. Einstein withdrew his doctoral thesis to get back the 230-franc submission fee. Along with whatever savings he had, the 230 francs would be enough money to keep a roof over his head for a few months.

The trio later dubbed themselves "The Olympia Academy." Over the years this informal gathering of minds, which saw members come and go, sat around Einstein's home dining on sausages, cheese, and fruit while discussing philosophy, science, and literature, to name just a few subjects. For Einstein, these gatherings were bliss. Aside from the sheer pleasure of listening or contributing to the theories, interpretations, and analyses by his young friends, there was another benefit: It challenged Einstein to more clearly develop his own ideas and determine the questions he would devote himself to pursuing.[10]

Einstein's money worries had become critical by the time spring arrived in Bern. He had not seen Maric in several months, who was suffering through her own difficulties in Novi Sad. Einstein's parents were still displeased at the prospect of having Maric as a daughter-in-law. Hermann was not in the best of health, and he worried about what was to become of his son. Perhaps to offset the stress, Einstein threw himself deeper into his research. He wrote letters to his dear friends Besso and Grossmann, sharing his thoughts and scientific theories, and kept them abreast of any news. Solovine and Habicht were also helpful sounding boards that enabled Einstein to clarify his thoughts before committing them to papers for possible publication.

Just as life was looking its bleakest, Einstein heard from the Swiss Patent Office. After interviewing with Haller, Einstein was told to start work on June 23, 1902. His salary, 3,500 francs a year, finally ended the constant worry of starving or being homeless. His friend Marcel Grossmann had been a "lifesaver" again, and Einstein acknowledged Grossmann's importance in his life, saying, "I might not have died, but I would have been intellectually stunted."[11]

At eight o'clock every morning, Einstein walked to the office, conveniently located just a few blocks away. Despite the long hours (he worked six days a week) plus private

ALBERT EINSTEIN AND HIS FIRST WIFE, MILEVA, CIRCA 1905.

As a patent examiner, Einstein may have found a good outlet to exercise his scientific imagination.

instruction (not having much engineering training, Einstein required some training from Haller) Einstein seemed to like his new post. He should not have liked Haller, though. Haller's strict instructions and authoritarian demeanor were much like his teachers in Germany, but Einstein thought his new boss "a splendid character and a clever mind."[12] Haller was very explicit in conveying his expectations of his patent examiners—to review all submitted inventions consistently through objective, substantiated measures that would hold up in court if legally challenged.

Although Einstein initially preferred trying to secure work in an academic environment, the role of patent examiner actually might have suited him better. His ability to create experiments in his imagination was well-suited to the mental perception of various inventions. As a patent examiner, therefore, Einstein may have found a good outlet to exercise his scientific imagination.[13]

Einstein embraced his new job with great enthusiasm, sharing the details of his work with his friends and Maric. Sitting on his work stool eight hours a day, he told how he sorted through the patent submissions, looking for those that had potential while setting aside those that showed no promise. Einstein particularly enjoyed analyzing the more imaginative and complex inventions. Usually, those inventors sent along a confusing or rather ambiguous description of their submissions. Einstein's approach was to make sense out of it all as though he were trying to decipher a code. He referred to this as "cobbling."

One of the intangibles of his job was that he was constantly exposed to a continuous stream of diverse creativity that spurred on his own intellectual thinking. His schedule also afforded him the opportunity to work on his own ideas, so this was a very productive period in his life. Einstein spent a total of seven years at the Swiss Patent Office and always remembered his time there fondly. Years later he wrote to his friend Besso, referring to the Office as "that temporal monastery, where I hatched my most beautiful ideas."[14] Of his work at the Office, Haller had only praises for young Einstein. He cited his quick grasp of the job, which enabled him to handle the more complex patent applications effectively, thereby making him "one of the most valued experts there."[15]

Now that Einstein had his professional life in order, it was time to address his personal situation, as well. He desperately wanted his parents' consent to marry Mileva Maric, and finally got his wish. Unfortunately, he finally got their blessing during a very painful time for the entire Einstein family. In the fall of 1902, Einstein learned that his father was very ill. The years of stress from failed businesses and financial problems had taken their toll on Hermann. Einstein left Bern to visit with his dying father in Milan. It was a difficult time for father and son, but Hermann finally gave his consent for Albert and Maric to marry. Fifty-five-year-old Hermann Einstein died on October 10. Hermann's death left Albert devastated, so much so that years later he wrote that it "was the deepest shock he had ever experienced."[16]

Einstein returned to Bern and sent for Maric. In a quiet ceremony at the registry office in Bern on January 6, 1903, the couple married. No one from either side of the family was in attendance, but friends Conrad Habicht and Maurice Solovine stood in as witnesses. After the ceremony, the four went out to dinner at a nearby restaurant. Unable to afford a honeymoon, the Einsteins returned to their apartment to settle into married life. If Einstein was troubled about his decision to marry, or the circumstances under which he received his father's consent, he did not share it with others. He wrote to Besso to tell him the news, assuring him that he was leading an enjoyable life with his new bride, and that his scientific work was also going quite well. At the time he wrote to Besso, Einstein could not have imagined how extraordinary the next few years would be.

CHAPTER FIVE

The Miracle Year of 1905

With Einstein settled in his job and finally married, many of the pressures he had been dealing with were finally dissipating. He and Mileva were reunited after having been apart almost a year. The Olympia Academy continued to meet regularly, providing an opportunity for Einstein and his friends to read and discuss books, including those by Ernst Mach, Henri Poincaré, and John Stuart Mill. Woven into their scientific explorations were literary readings by such notables as Sophocles, Dickens, and Cervantes.

The Swiss Patent Office became a kind of oasis for Einstein. He found his work stimulating, and with a steady paycheck, his mind was relieved of the financial worries that had plagued him for so long. By June, he and Mileva had saved enough money to go away on a belated honeymoon. They traveled to Lausanne, a port city in western Switzerland on Lake Geneva. Shortly after, Mileva made a visit to her parents in Novi Sad. Einstein returned to Bern and his job at the Patent Office. While still at her parents' home, Mileva discovered that she was pregnant again and wrote Einstein to share the news. He was delighted and encouraged her to return home soon.

The early years in Bern were among the most enjoyable and productive in Einstein's life. He continued to find his work interesting and rewarding. Many years after he had left the Patent Office, Einstein continued to maintain an interest in the inventions of technology. "I . . . never ceased to concern myself with technical matters. This was of benefit also to my scientific research," said Einstein.[1] In his free time, Einstein devoted much of his thoughts and energies to the issues of physics that seemed to hold a constant fascination for him. It was during this time that Einstein began a concentrated period of theorizing, writing, and reflection on a variety of scientific topics, including his continued interest in the behavior of atoms and molecules when exposed to heat (thermodynamics).

Einstein also discovered a colleague at the office—Dr. Josef Sauter—who had studied at the Polytechnic and served as chief assistant to physics professor Heinrich Weber. Sauter was eight years older than Einstein, which explained why their paths had not crossed at the Institute. Like Einstein, Sauter sought to learn more about physics than was covered in the ETH curriculum. Because Sauter read and studied the works of James Clerk Maxwell and Hermann von Helmholtz, Einstein was able to discuss theories on thermodynamics with him. Sauter was a welcome colleague and friend. He read some of Einstein's papers on thermodynamics and even found some errors, which Einstein gratefully corrected.

Sauter was well connected with the scientific community

in Bern, and introduced many of those colleagues to Einstein, opening a whole new arena of intellectuals with whom to share his own thoughts and ideas. Sauter also took Einstein as his guest to a meeting of the *Naturforschende Gesellschaft* (Natural Science Society), an organization of members in a variety of professions including professors, teachers, and notable individuals in the fields of medicine and pharmacology. Einstein himself was named a member of the Society in May and gave his first lecture, on "The Theory of Electromagnetic Waves," that December.

Einstein continued to work on his analysis of thermodynamics, writing a paper on the *General Molecular Theory of Heat*, which was published in the *Annalen* in the spring of 1904. A few months later, Einstein again became a father with the birth of his son, Hans Albert, on May 14. Einstein's close friend, Michele Besso, applied for an opening as a Technical Expert II Class in the Swiss Patent Office. He was chosen among thirteen applicants and moved to Bern in the summer.

Although Einstein did not receive a promotion, he did earn "permanent" status and a raise that brought his salary to 3,900 francs a year (approximately $2,689). With his closest friend working in the same office, Einstein always had someone near to discuss ideas with. He and Besso often walked home from work together, engrossed in some scientific discussion, just enjoying each other's company.

All Einstein's reading, discussions, and theorizing about the physical world seemed to peak in 1905, the year in Einstein's life that is referred to as *Annus Mirabilis* (miracle year). Of this breakthrough in his thinking, Einstein said it was as if "a storm broke loose in my mind."[2] Only twenty-six years old, with a lifetime of exploration and discovery still ahead of him, Einstein already had significant theories germinating in his mind. Within a span of a few months, he wrote four papers that were published in the *Annalen der Physik*.

The content of these papers would transform the way the scientific community and the world would view the universe. Einstein's theories are all very complex, and hundreds of essays have been written about them in an attempt to explain them so both professionals and laypeople can understand them. Of understanding the importance and the consequences of his contribution, Einstein said, "What is essential in the life of a man of my kind lies in *what* he thinks and *how* he thinks, and not in what he does or suffers."[3]

Before they were even in print, an enthusiastic Einstein wrote a brief description of the contents of the papers to his friend Conrad Habicht:

> [The first] is on the radiation and energy of light, and it is very revolutionary. . . . The second discusses the methods of determining the real dimensions of atoms by investigating the diffusion and internal friction of liquid solutions. The third proves that, according to the molecular theory of heat, bodies of dimensions of the order of 1/1000 mm. suspended in liquid experience apparent random movement due to the thermal motion of molecules. . . . The fourth work is based on the concepts of electrodynamics of moving bodies and modifies the theory of space and time."[4]

The first paper addressed the phenomenon known as

the photoelectric effect, or the release of electrons (very small negatively charged particles) from metal when light is shone on it. Building on the ideas of Max Planck, Einstein proposed that light was made up of individual bundles of energy or quanta (photons), which interacted with the electrons in the metal like distinct particles, rather than as continuous waves. It was from the work in this paper that Einstein would be awarded the Nobel Prize in Physics in 1922.

Einstein's other significant papers that year included one in which he developed a mathematical theory to explain the visible motion of particles suspended in a liquid ("On the Motion—Required by the Molecular Kinetic Theory of Heat—of Small Particles Suspended in a Stationary Liquid"), and his most famous and controversial paper on the theory of relativity ("On the Electrodynamics of Moving Bodies"). In this paper, Einstein theorized that if the speed of light is constant and if all natural laws are identical for all observers moving relative to each other at constant speed, then the passage of time and the measurement of lengths would have to be relative to the observer.

This paper was most astonishing because it seemed to contradict scientist Sir Isaac Newton's long-standing hypothesis that space and time are absolute—the same for all observers. Einstein's theory was very radical for its time because in their research, scientists are always looking for things that are "constant." By searching for the "constants" in things, it is easier to discover the things that *do* change. The foundation of Einstein's theory of relativity was based on the supposition that light always travels for all observers at 186,000 miles per second.

Albert Einstein is pictured here during the "Miracle Year" of 1905.

Prior to Einstein's theory, science worked on the accepted natural laws established by Newton and the Italian astronomer Galileo—that in an orderly, mechanical universe, the speed of light is added to the speed of motion. In his book, *Albert Einstein and the Theory of Relativity*, author Robert Cwiklik further explains:

> Galileo had said, and Newton had confirmed, that in a mechanical universe, speeds add up. That is, if one shines a light from a car moving at 60 miles per hour, for example, the speed of the car would be added to the speed of the light and make it faster. . . . Light does not obey Newton's law of the addition of velocities—it always moves at the same speed.[5]

In a continuation of his new theory, Einstein discovered "the equivalence of mass and energy, according to which the energy *E* of a quantity of matter, with mass *m*, is equal to the product of the mass and the square of the velocity of light, *c*."[6] In this theory, Einstein was stating that mass is equivalent to a certain amount of energy. In order to find a mass's energy equivalent, you have to multiply the speed of light by itself and then by the mass. Because the speed of light is so incredibly large (186,000 mps), squaring it and then multiplying the result by even the smallest mass will produce a massive amount of energy. Einstein's special theory of relativity gave rise to the famous equation, $E = mc^2$.

Einstein was actually rather casual about his newfound discoveries. Besso, who Einstein had said was "an ideal soundingboard" had spent many hours with Einstein, listening to him as he tried to discover the truth about the laws of the universe.[7] According to author Banesh Hoffmann:

> Einstein said his basic discovery came on waking up one morning, when he suddenly saw the idea. This had been going around and around at the back of his mind for years, and suddenly it wanted to thrust itself forward into his conscious mind.[8]

Despite the fact that he had been mulling over these thoughts for a while and talking them out with Besso, on that eventful morning Einstein only casually mentioned his spectacular discovery to him saying, "Thank you. I've completely solved the problem. An analysis of the concept of time was my solution. Time cannot be absolutely defined, and there is an inseparable relation between time and signal velocity."[9]

Einstein anticipated that his papers would stir interest and cause controversy in the scientific community, and eagerly awaited reaction. Much to his dismay, by year's end there had been very little. And yet Einstein's view of space and time was very significant. His theory came at a time when scientists were beginning to "think outside the box." Astronomers were trying to learn more about space beyond our galaxy. Scientists in general were realizing that they were able to understand only a tiny part about our complex universe. Perhaps the significance of Einstein's theories was in his timing—imagining possibilities when scientists were looking for explanations beyond what had been the accepted laws from the work of Sir Isaac Newton.

Although Einstein was a little bit disappointed by the lack of initial interest in his published papers, he realized that he still needed to conduct actual laboratory experiments to test his theories. He also had not taken into account the delay between his papers being published in *Annalen* and his colleagues having an opportunity to react to his extraordinary theories. Scientists are not in the habit of ignoring research; they are just sometimes slow to respond. Eventually, the scientific community did begin to react. Some accepted Einstein's ideas enthusiastically, some tentatively. Others firmly rejected the suppositions expressed in his papers, but Einstein's colleagues did not ignore his work.

> *"What is essential in the life of a man of my kind lies in* what *he thinks and* how *he thinks, not in what he does or suffers."*
>
> **—Albert Einstein**

Einstein was never a very patient man and his mind was rarely, if ever, absent of thoughts for very long. Having submitted the flurry of papers to *Annalen*, Einstein turned his attention to other endeavors. Earlier in the year, he had resumed interest in acquiring his Ph.D. A few years before he had given up the idea of acquiring his Ph.D., once saying, "this doesn't help me much and the whole comedy has begun to bore me."[10] However, he had not given up on the desire to one day become a professor, and a Ph.D. was a prerequisite for any career in academia. It also certainly could not hurt in his current post at the Patent Office.

He first submitted his newly written paper on the *Electrodynamics of Moving Bodies* to the "decision-making" members of the faculty at the Zurich Polytechnic. However, his theory of relativity was so new and so radical that it was rejected. So instead, Einstein went through his other writings and put together a paper he entitled *On a New Determination of Molecular Dimensions*. This paper addressed the definite existence and movement of molecules in a water mixture. This paper was accepted and Einstein was awarded his Ph.D. in January 1906. He could now claim the new title, Herr Doktor Einstein.

By the spring of 1906, Einstein's published papers were finally attracting attention. Much to Einstein's pleasure, acknowledgement of his relativity theory came from a prominent member of the scientific community—German physicist Max Planck. Another future recipient of the Nobel Prize in Physics, Planck had done his own research on the behavior of light and energy, and had postulated his own ideas on the subject. Planck's work had been groundbreaking because it shattered many of the previous notions about the nature of the physical world. Before then, it had been widely accepted that light, heat, and other forms of radiation moved in streams. But Planck showed this radiation actually moved in separate bundles of energy, which he called *quanta* (which is Latin for "how much").[11]

Einstein was well aware of Planck's contributions to the world of physics and was delighted when he saw Planck's name and return address on an envelope as he was sorting through his mail. He expected the letter to be full of criticism about his published papers in *Annalen*, but was pleasantly surprised when he began reading Planck's note:

> I have read with great interest your papers in the *Annalen der Physik* on the Theory of Relativity and the Photoelectric Effect. I must say I am fascinated and energized by your application of the speed of light as a universal constant. However, there are some questions I should be pleased for you to answer concerning some of your ideas.[12]

Planck's letter was an exciting validation for Einstein and his work. The renowned physicist from Berlin, Germany, found Einstein's work inspiring. If Planck thought there were merits in Einstein's theories, surely other physicists would, too.

Max Planck quickly emerged as a great advocate of Einstein's theory of relativity. Because he was so interested in pursuing what Einstein had introduced, Planck's role in promoting and further developing the relativity theory was enormously significant. Planck's interest spilled over into discussions with other colleagues, and in his lectures as physics professor at the University of Berlin.

It was because of Planck's standing in the scientific community and his continuation of Einstein's work that the relativity theory was so quickly accepted. Several years later, Einstein acknowledged Planck's importance and expressed his gratitude by writing, "It is largely due to the determined and cordial manner in which he [Planck] supported this theory that it attracted notice so quickly among my colleagues in the field."[13]

The year 1905 had indeed been a momentous year for both Patent Office Expert Class III Herr Einstein and the world of science. The twenty-seven-year-old physicist was about to go from obscurity in Bern, Switzerland, to world recognition.

CHAPTER SIX

AMONG THE SCIENTIFIC ELITE

While the scientific community outside of Bern was absorbing the contents of Einstein's papers and was abuzz about their implications, the only noticeable change within Einstein's Bern circle of friends and colleagues was that he had earned his doctorate and was now referred to as Herr Doktor. Einstein was suddenly being met with congratulatory greetings for the accomplishment, which he seemed to enjoy, he said, because, "In my experience, it quite considerably facilitates relations with people."[1]

Einstein's newly acquired doctorate status was also noted in his application for a promotion in the Patent Office to the Swiss Federal Council. In the spring of 1906 Expert Class III Einstein was upgraded to Expert Class II and received a raise, boosting his salary to 4,500 francs a year ($3,062). Although Einstein was pleased with the fact that he was getting a raise, he was never really satisfied with his salary at the Patent Office, and from time to time sought employment elsewhere.

Having never fully given up on the idea of working in academia, Einstein began looking for a teaching post. After receiving a doctoral degree, the next step toward a professorship was to become a *privatdozent* (a non-salaried, apprentice lecturer at a university). The prerequisite for consideration to such an appointment was the completion of a *Habilitation*, a procedure that required the submission of an original thesis and conducting a trial lecture. Einstein decided to reapply to the University of Bern in 1908 (he had been turned down in 1903). After completing the requirements to the satisfaction of the faculty, Einstein started his first academic job as a privatdozent for theoretical physics. Because it was a non-paying job, Einstein had to keep his post at the Patent Office.

Einstein's first class in the summer of 1908 consisted of three students—co-workers and friends at the Patent Office, Michele Besso and Heinrich Schenk, and Lucien Chavan, another friend of Einstein's who worked at the Postal and Telegraph Administration. In keeping with Einstein's current physics investigations, the class discussed the molecular theory of heat. For the winter semester, with the addition of new student Max Stern, the class discussed theories on radiation. In whatever free time Einstein had between his class, his job at the Patent Office, and being a husband and father, he also continued to write papers and conduct experiments related to his relativity theory.

Einstein's work got an endorsement from an unexpected source—his former mathematics professor at the

Polytechnic, Hermann Minkowski. While lecturing in Göttingen at the end of 1907, Minkowski took Einstein's theory to the next level. In his own presentation, he expounded on its importance by introducing a fourth dimension known as space-time. "From now on," he said, "space and time separately have vanished into the merest shadows, and only a sort of combination of the two preserves any reality."[2]

Minkowski advanced Einstein's work to a more extensive professional audience less than a year later at a conference in Cologne, Germany. When members of the *Deutsche Gesellschaft der Naturforscher und Ärzte* (the German Society of Scientists and Physicians) gathered in September 1908, Minkowski continued to laud the importance of Einstein's work. Unable to attend the convention himself, Einstein missed Minkowski's presentation on his mathematical interpretation of Einstein's theory of relativity through the use of geometry. As excited as Minkowski was about Einstein's work, the two never had the chance to meet again because Mankowski died four months later.

As Einstein's reputation grew, many in the scientific community wondered why he was working in the Patent Office in Bern instead of teaching at a university. One of the difficulties Einstein faced in trying to get into a paying academic position was there really were no openings for a physicist with his specialty. However, his former academic advisor on his doctoral thesis, Alfred Kleiner, finally provided that opportunity. After much discussion among the cantonal education authorities, a post was created for a theoretical physicist at the University of Zurich. Kleiner's first choice was Friedrich Adler, a former schoolmate and friend of Einstein's at the ETH. Adler, however, felt that Einstein was much more deserving of the post, as he indicated in a letter to his father:

> For the people involved the situation is of course that, on the one hand, they have a bad conscience about the way they treated him in the past, and on the other it is felt to be a scandal, not only here but also in Germany, that a man like that should sit in the Patent Office.[3]

After a vote among the professors of Science Section II, Einstein was confirmed to the post of extraordinary professor of theoretical physics. On May 7, 1909, the Governmental Council of the Canton of Zurich approved Einstein's appointment. He would begin his position at the beginning of the winter session on October 15, 1909.

Einstein almost overlooked his first honorary degree. Forty years later he recalled the rather amusing incident by explaining: "One day I received a large envelope at the Patent Office, containing an elegant sheet of paper with some words in picturesque print (I even believe in Latin) which seemed to me impersonal and of little interest, and therefore landed at once in the official wastepaper basket."[4] It was not until later when he talked to Louis Chavan, who was asked by the authorities at Geneva University to convince Einstein to travel to Geneva, that he learned what the mail was about.

Geneva University was celebrating its 350th anniversary by its founder, reformationist John Calvin, and invited Einstein to join the celebration. During the festivities, the plan was to award Einstein an honorary doctorate. Einstein did arrive in time to participate in the July celebration, and later received the unexpected honorary degree along with such other distinguished European scientists as chemist Ernest Solvay and 1903 Physics Nobel Prize co-recipient Marie Sklodowska Curie. The celebration concluded with a rather lavish feast, the likes of which Einstein had never experienced.

Two months later, Einstein gave his first major lecture, which he presented at the first international physics conference in Salzburg, Austria. Leading scientists in attendance included Max Planck, Max Born, and Arnold Sommerfeld. Many had anticipated a talk from Einstein about his relativity theory, but as Born noted, "[Einstein] had already proceeded beyond Special Relativity which he left to minor prophets, while he pondered about the new riddles arising from the quantum structure of light, and of course about gravitation and General Relativity."[5]

For his lecture, Einstein instead chose to talk about his most recent interest, *The Nature and Constitution of Radiation*. Einstein envisioned that it would be determined that light would be found in both wave and particle form. "It cannot be denied that there exists a large group of radiation-related facts which show that light possesses certain fundamental properties which can much more easily be understood from the standpoint of wave theory," Einstein explained.[6]

Although his colleagues were skeptical about the idea of light as both waves and particles, it was a historic appearance for Einstein and the members of the scientific community in attendance. Again, colleague Max Born echoed Einstein's importance in the field. Another colleague, Wolfgang Pauli, as much as two decades later, also commented on Einstein's Salzburg appearance, saying that his lecture could be "seen as one of the turning points in the evolution of theoretical physics."[7]

Albert, Mileva, and Hans Albert moved to Zurich in October in time to get settled before Einstein began his first semester at the university. He liked his new position, but found his new job was more demanding of his time than his employment at the Patent Office in Bern had been. Einstein shared his initial impressions with friend and colleague Jakob Laub, "My new profession is very much to my liking. I am on very close terms with my students and hope I'll be able to give some ideas to some of them."[8]

Einstein's workload consisted of six hours of classroom time plus one evening seminar. Between the time spent in class and preparation time, Einstein actually had less free time to devote to his own work than he had in Bern. He was also really a novice at the lectern, and his appearance was rather casual, if not unkempt. He hardly looked the part of a university professor—coming to class wearing somewhat wrinkled pants that were too short, hair tousled, and grasping a small scrap of paper that turned out to contain the major points he wished to cover in the day's lecture.

Despite his outward appearance, Einstein's students warmed to him almost immediately. His informal teaching style included encouraging his students to interrupt him during his lectures if something was not being understood. During breaks, students gathered around him asking a barrage of questions that Einstein patiently attempted to address. It was not uncommon for Einstein to invite students to join him at the Terrasse Café after the evening class to continue discussions. Sometimes, to Mileva's dismay, her husband even brought a group of students back to their already cramped apartment. Things at home became even more strained when Mileva gave birth to their second child, Eduard, on July 28, 1910.

The year 1910 also marked the first time Einstein was nominated for the Nobel Prize in Physics. The nomination came from Wilhelm Ostwald, a renowned professor and recipient of the Nobel Prize in Chemistry the previous year. Ironically, Ostwald had rejected Einstein's appeal to become his assistant in 1901 when he was seeking a job after graduating from the Polytechnic.

Despite the fact that professionally and personally Einstein's life seemed harmonious and productive, he recognized that in his post as *Extraordinarius* at the university he was not an equal member of the faculty. Even though he and Mileva liked Zurich, Einstein accepted the fact that at some point he would probably have to leave to better his position and salary. He did not have to wait long. Having been on the job less than six months in Zurich, Einstein was approached about a full professorship at the German University in Prague.

Today, Prague is the capital city of the Czech Republic, but in the early 1900s, Prague was part of the Austrian Empire. Despite the opportunity for Einstein to enhance his professional status, the appointment was not without its problems. There were political considerations—what was the feasibility of a German-born Jew with Swiss citizenship being appointed to a post at a German institution in an Austrian city?

Einstein's decision as a youngster to abandon his religious affiliation complicated matters because Austrian Emperor Franz Josef required all university employees to be members of a recognized religion. In order to satisfy Josef's condition, Einstein wrote *Mosaisch* (the Austrian word for Jewish) in the religion space on the application form. In a letter dated August 24, 1911, Einstein wrote to his friend and colleague Heinrich Zangger (professor of forensic medicine at the University of Zurich and founder of emergency medicine):

> Dressed in a most picturesque uniform, I took the solemn oath of office in front of the viceroy of Bohemia yesterday, putting to use my Jewish "faith," which I put on again for this purpose. It was a comical scene.[9]

Even though Einstein had come to distrust all forms of organized religion, he could not escape the prejudice and hatred others harbored in various parts of Europe against Jews. This was particularly true in Germany, Austria, and other eastern European countries. As a result, Einstein would eventually find himself drawn to the Jewish community, which included several professionals and laypeople involved in the Zionist movement—individuals who were attempting to establish a Jewish state. Einstein never became a Zionist, but he was sympathetic to the plight of Jews, and had to deal with anti-Semitism because of his religious origins.

Before Einstein moved his family to Prague to begin his professorship at the German University in the spring of 1911, he and Mileva traveled to Leyden, the Netherlands, at the invitation of Hendrik Antoon Lorentz, a well-respected mathematical physicist who refined James Maxwell's electromagnetic theory. Lorentz proposed that light waves were created by fluctuations of an electric charge in an atom. Einstein considered Lorentz his "scientific father figure," and was pleased by the opportunity to appear as a guest lecturer and visit with Lorentz.

It was a delightful encounter for Einstein, who chatted with Lorentz and other colleagues, including Heike Kamerlingh Onnes and Willem Hendrik Keesom. In 1928, at Lorentz's funeral, Einstein spoke about the man who had meant so much to him in life:

> [His] unfailing kindness and generosity, his sense of justice, combined with an intuitive insight into people and conditions, made him a leader wherever he found himself. Everyone followed him gladly, because they felt that he never wanted to dominate them, but always only to serve them.[10]

The Einsteins arrived in Prague on April 1, 1911. Although Einstein found the German University and his work there pleasant enough, it was not too long before he became well aware of the conflict between the Czechs and the Germans. The Germans refused to speak Czech and the Czechs refused to speak German, resisting the political, economic, and social control of the Germans. Everything seemed divided, including the educational institutions, which had split over their nationality and language divergences. Einstein quickly discovered that there was also little scientific stimulation in Prague, but found solace in the University's library, which gave him the "chance of indulging, without interruption," his scientific reflection.[11]

In less than six months, Einstein found that even the library was not enough to keep him content in Prague. There were countless bureaucratic meetings, endless amounts of paperwork, and students who were nowhere near as enthusiastic or hard-working as their counterparts in

Zurich. Once again Einstein had no reluctance about moving on if another professional opportunity emerged.

To keep himself occupied, Einstein continued to muse over the mysteries of the quantum theory. He also was preparing a paper that he would read at a scientific conference. Scientist Walther Nernst and Belgian businessman and philanthropist Ernest Solvay organized the first Solvay Congress, held in Brussels, Belgium, from October 30 to November 4. The conference was designed to bring together the scientific intellectual élite to further discuss radiation and quantum theory. Twenty of the most influential scientists in Europe were invited, including former and future Nobel Prize recipients like Marie Curie, Ernest Rutherford, Max Planck, Henri Poincaré, and Hendrik Lorentz.

By the very presence of many of the participants, the conference received a great deal of publicity. Einstein's reputation was spreading throughout the science community in Europe, and offers of the academic opportunities Einstein sought for so long began to multiply. He met with officials at the University of Utrecht in Holland, where Lorentz taught. There were also opportunities in Vienna, and even in the United States at Columbia University in New York.

However, Einstein really wanted to return to Zurich. Mileva was unhappy in Prague, Einstein found his work unfulfilling, and exciting things were happening at his alma mater. The Polytechnic had been upgraded to the *Eidgenössische Technische Universitat* (the Swiss Federal Technical University), which meant it now had full academic status, including a doctoral program. As a result of the necessity to reorganize academic departments, his old friend Marcel Grossmann had been named dean of the math and science division. With help from Grossmann and Zangger and favorable recommendations from Marie Curie and Henri Poincaré, on January 30, 1912, Einstein was elected professor of physics at the Swiss Technical University.

After giving his notice at the German University, the Einsteins began preparing to move back to Zurich over the summer. Although delighted with his new appointment, Einstein made a trip to Berlin around the Easter holiday to meet with Nernst, Planck, Emil Warburg, chemist Fritz Haber, and astronomer Erwin Freundlich. Nernst and Planck were anxious to convince their German-born colleague to return to Germany, but the idea of going back to the country and the culture Einstein found so distasteful as a youth had not changed. However, while in Berlin, Einstein also visited with Elsa Löwenthal, a cousin he had not seen since he was a child living in Munich.

Divorced with two daughters, Ilse and Margot, Elsa and the girls were living in a nice top-floor apartment in Berlin. Elsa's parents, Rudolf and Fanny Einstein, were also living in the building. Einstein was directly related to his Aunt Fanny—she was Pauline Einstein's sister. Einstein's own marriage had been deteriorating and he found himself attracted to Elsa. Even though Einstein knew he and his wife were drifting apart, he was in no position to court Elsa. The two enjoyed each other's company for the few days they had together in Berlin, and then Einstein went back to Prague.

Having met Elsa, Einstein no longer thought of living in Berlin as quite so awful. And even though he discouraged

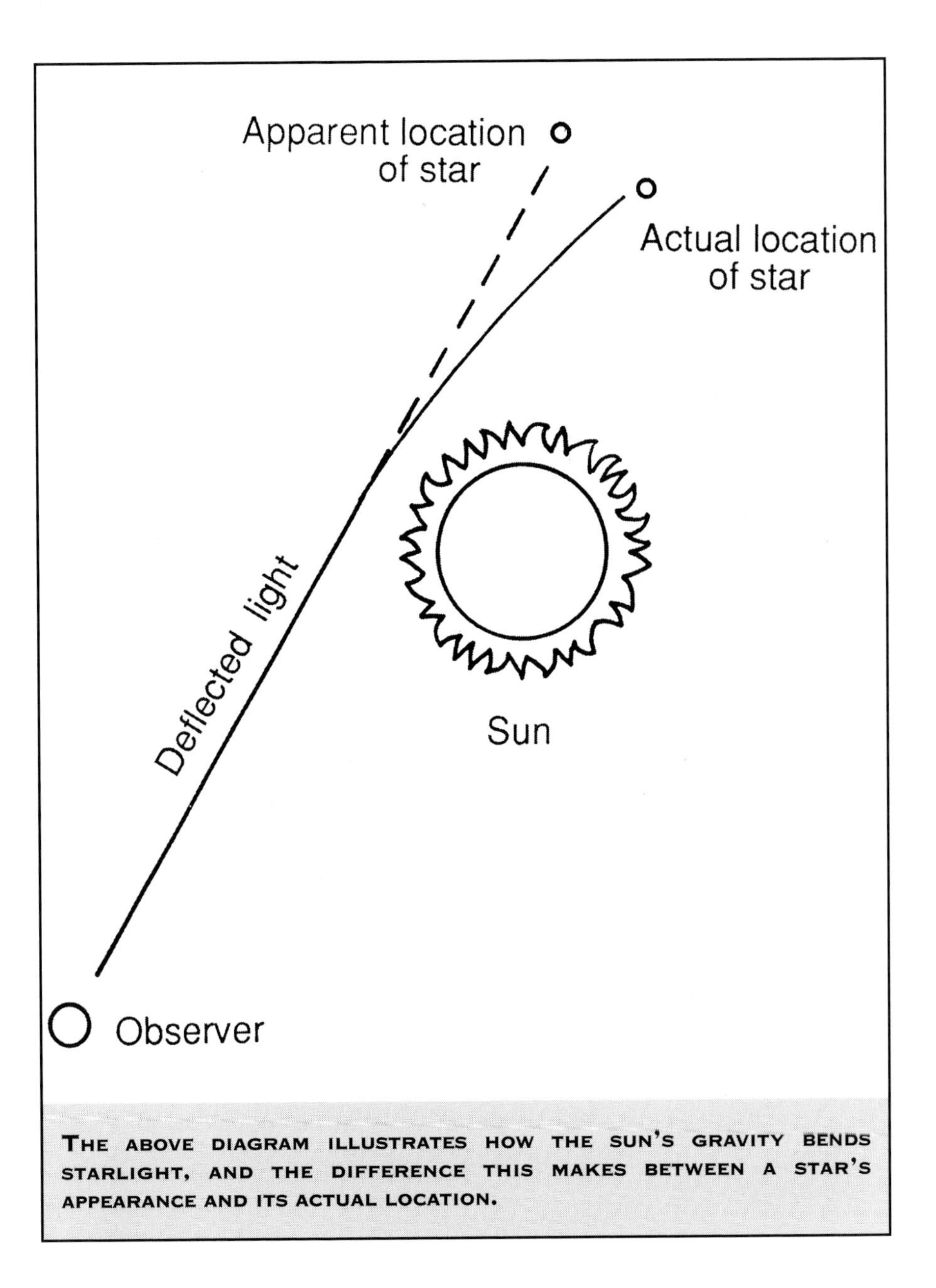

THE ABOVE DIAGRAM ILLUSTRATES HOW THE SUN'S GRAVITY BENDS STARLIGHT, AND THE DIFFERENCE THIS MAKES BETWEEN A STAR'S APPEARANCE AND ITS ACTUAL LOCATION.

any continuation of contact with Elsa, the two corresponded by mail. Because Mileva was a very jealous woman, Einstein had Elsa mail her letters to a different address in Zurich.

During his brief tenure at the Swiss Federal Technical University, Einstein continued to work on gravity's influence on the diffusion of light. Einstein theorized that light rays passing near the sun were deflected by the sun's gravitational field. As a result a star, which appears to be near the sun, seems to increase its angular distance from the sun. This point was important because the curvature of starlight by the sun is a key prediction of general relativity. It would be the confirmation of this belief that would validate the general theory of relativity.

To test this theory, Einstein concluded that if the sky seen behind the sun during a solar eclipse was photographed and then compared to photographs taken of a normal night sky, the small deflection of light would be revealed as an arc in the eclipse photo. Astronomer Erwin Freundlich was very enthusiastic about assisting Einstein and testing the theory. Unfortunately, the next solar eclipse was not due to occur until September 1914 in southern Russia. Regretfully, Einstein and Freundlich would have to wait a while, because the First World War broke out before the eclipse took place.

As Einstein had done so often in his academic career, he was no sooner settled at the Swiss Federal Technical University when he began thinking about opportunities elsewhere. In July 1913, Einstein was visited by Nernst and Planck, who were prepared to present to their extraordinary colleague a very attractive offer that awaited him in Berlin. The Prussian scientific community recognized that the addition of Einstein would add a great deal of prestige to Prussia and the Prussian Academy.[12]

Planck and Nernst came with a deal too good to turn down. Einstein would be made a professor at the University of Berlin without having to give lectures or seminars unless he chose to do so. In addition, he would be named the director of the Institute of Theoretical Physics within the Kaiser Wilhelm Society, and given membership in the Prussian Academy of Science. Einstein's feelings about his native home had not changed, but the professional rewards, including the opportunity to work with some of the best minds in the field of physics, and being near Pauline and Elsa, may have softened his bad memories of Germany.

To understand the enormity of the offer, one only need look at Einstein the man as a candidate. He was certainly not the most optimal candidate in the eyes of Germany's ruler Kaiser Wilhelm II. Einstein was first and foremost a Jew; he had renounced his German citizenship; and he had never served in the Prussian military. Nonetheless, Einstein's position in the world of science was important enough to overlook these obvious drawbacks. They were happy to have him, and Einstein, without even consulting Mileva, accepted the offer.

Einstein's decision to go to Berlin only added to the deterioration of his marriage. He had not considered the impact that moving closer to his mother would have on Mileva. Pauline had never accepted Mileva as a daughter-in-law and the two had never gotten along. The decision to accept the invitation to Berlin was met with puzzlement by some of his friends and colleagues. As a youngster, he had hated the very educational system his sons would be subjected to.

Some Einstein historians speculate that Einstein put aside his distaste for Germany in order to be united with the very people—Germans—from whom he had received his earliest recognition. Einstein expressed his gratitude to Planck for his support of the relativity theory in a tribute to Planck when he said, "The notice which this theory encountered so quickly among my fellow scientists is largely due to the determination and warmth with which he championed this theory."[13]

Einstein may have actually had a much simpler reason for accepting his new appointment. In a letter to his friend Paul Ehrenfest, Einstein wrote that lecturing was getting on his nerves and in Berlin he would have no obligations eating away at his time, which he preferred spending pondering about the universe. And of course Elsa was in Berlin. Einstein had continued his correspondence with her and she was among the first with whom he shared the news of his appointment to the University of Berlin.

In February, Einstein made his farewells to his colleagues in Zurich. Despite her protests and misgivings about Berlin, Mileva had traveled there to secure an apartment. Mileva felt sure she would never be comfortable in Berlin, and thus would not remain there long. Mileva was right—just a few months later, Michele Besso came to Berlin to help move her and the boys back to Switzerland.

Einstein had moved into his new home in April 1914. It was here that he would remain for the next nineteen years.

CHAPTER SEVEN

AN OUTSIDER IN BERLIN

Outside the insulated world of scientific exploration, debate, and discovery, political tensions among several countries, including Austria, Serbia, Germany, Russia, and Britain finally erupted into war.

It began as a conflict between Austria-Hungary and Serbia on July 28, 1914, but quickly expanded a month later when Germany declared war on Russia and France. When Germany invaded Belgium for military access to France, Britain declared war on Germany, igniting World War I. Known as the Great War, World War I was a four-year-long grueling and costly conflict fought in the endless trenches across Europe that resulted in more than 8 million deaths and incalculable destruction.

Inexplicable enthusiasm for the war erupted among all societal classes. Caught in the midst of this roiling turmoil was Albert Einstein—pacifist and internationalist. He had long ago developed a revulsion for militarism and all its components, including aggression, weapons, and lethal intent. Einstein's acute aversion extended to all things competitive, like sports and even board games like chess.

The war was supposed to be a quick and victorious one for Germany. When that did not happen, many of Germany's best and brightest, scientists and intellectuals alike, felt that it was imperative to champion the cause of Germany to the international community. A document called the "Manifesto to the Civilized World" (later nicknamed the Manifesto of the 93) was drafted by German writer Ludwig Fulda and signed by ninety-three well-respected scholars throughout the Prussian empire. The manifesto protested "the lies and defamations with which our enemies are trying to besmirch Germany's pure cause in the hard life-and-death struggle forced upon it."[1]

Among the ninety-three signatures were those of painter Max Liebermann, poet Gerhart Hauptmann, evolutionist Ernst Haeckel, biologist Paul Ehrlich, and scientists Philipp Lenard, Wilhelm Röntgen, Walther Nernst, Fritz Haber, and Max Planck. Shortly after the release of the Manifesto of the 93, University of Berlin professor of physiology George Nicolai drafted a countermanifesto. It is not clear what role Einstein played in the writing of the "Manifesto to Europeans," but in a letter from Nicolai to Einstein several years later, Nicolai wrote, "Indeed, without your participation it might never have seen the light of day."[2]

The countermanifesto certainly was written in a tone that Einstein the pacifist would echo throughout the rest of his life. The document, which only managed to secure four signatures, began:

> Never before has any war so completely disrupted cultural cooperation. It has done so at the very time

> when progress in technology and communications clearly suggest that we recognize the need for international relations which will necessarily move in the direction of a universal, worldwide civilization. . . . [The] struggle raging today can scarcely yield a "victor"; all nations that participate in it will, in all likelihood, pay an exceedingly high price. . . .[3]

The legacy of World War I certainly reflects the sentiment expressed in the countermanifesto.

Within the "Manifesto to Europeans" there was a call to create a League of Europeans with the intent of organizing an extensive movement for European unity by those who agreed with the document's message. Despite his disdain for matters of politics, Einstein was persuaded to join the *Bund Neues Vaterland* (League of the New Fatherland), a political party "dedicated to peace and the prevention of future wars."[4] Had Einstein not been a Swiss citizen, several of his colleagues might have considered him a traitor in his homeland.

Because of his anti-war stance, Einstein also found himself rather isolated from his German colleagues. With Mileva and the boys back in Zurich, and his apartment scaled down to only the barest necessities, he led a tranquil but rather lonely existence. If he wanted company, however, he only had to make the fifteen-minute walk to Löwenthal's apartment, where he was assured a comfortable visit and a good home-cooked meal. He continued to view his nationalist-fevered colleagues with disappointment, and was even moved to feelings of disgust at the hypocrisy of men such as Nernst and Haber. Instead of using their brilliant minds to work on research for the betterment of humanity, they were busy helping to develop chemical weapons, including deadly mustard gas. All the while, men like Nernst and Haber accused the enemy of not fighting fairly in the war.

The war troubled Einstein for the course of its duration. Other than his scientific musings, his discomfort with what was going on around him occupied his thoughts, sometimes distracting him from his work. Einstein never wavered in his deep-held convictions about the business of war, and was much more outspoken about his disdain with friends who were likewise sympathetic, as demonstrated in this letter he wrote to Ehrenfest:

> The international catastrophe weighs heavily on me as an internationalist person. It is hard to understand, as one lives through this "great epoch," that one belongs to this crazy degenerate species that claims to possess freedom of will. If only somewhere there was an island for the benign and prudent! There I too would be a fervent patriot.[5]

During the first few years of the war, Einstein used the time to review what he had achieved with his theory of gravitation without having the experimental data from a solar eclipse. He desperately wanted to bring his theory to a conclusion and spent a great deal of time checking his previous work and approaching his hypotheses differently each time he set out to finish the puzzle. Over the summer of 1915, Einstein wanted to travel to Zurich, primarily to spend some time with his children. The visit with Hans and Eduard was delayed a bit, so Einstein used the time to vacation on the Baltic island of Rügen with Elsa Löwenthal and her daughters. In September, Einstein finally got to spend some time with his children, even taking Hans Albert hiking and boating.

When he returned to Berlin, he was almost consumed by his desire to unravel the nature of the universe and the part gravity played in it. He often skipped meals and stayed up late in the evenings. Finally, sometime in November, Einstein realized that he had found the answer he was looking for. To grasp Einstein's notion of space-time, you must be able to imagine the way he envisioned the universe, forgetting for a moment the idea that gravity is a force pulling between two objects. Author John Severance, in his book *Einstein: Visionary Scientist*, provided a visual description:

> [Imagine] space-time two dimensionally, as a taut sheet of rubber rather like a trampoline. A heavy bowling ball placed in its middle would, of course, cause a deep sag. A golf ball rolling by would be diverted from its straight path and start to orbit the bowling ball in its depression. In the universe, space-time is warped in a similar way, which is why the moon orbits the earth and the earth, in its turn, orbits the sun.[6]

Einstein believed that this was also true of light as it passes near celestial bodies. Einstein wrote about this in a paper called "The Foundation of the General Theory of Relativity," which was published in the *Annalen der Physik* in the spring of 1916.

Having finally achieved in his general theory of relativity what has been described as "the supreme intellectual achievement of the human species," Einstein spent days in a state of exhilarated joy.[7] He described his theory as his "most beautiful discovery." He only hoped that at some point astronomers would have the opportunity to observe a

A map showing the boundaries of Europe prior to World War I.

solar eclipse and to test what his calculations and math were telling him.

While the war raged, Einstein had his own personal battle with Mileva, which came to a head during Easter 1916, when he asked her for a divorce. She had hoped for a reconciliation, and would not agree to a dissolution of the marriage. A furious Einstein, believing that his children really did not want to see their father, determined never to see his wife again. Not long after his unpleasant encounter with Mileva, Einstein was contacted by friends Besso and Zangger and told that she had become seriously ill. Both friends suspected that Einstein's behavior had contributed to Mileva's condition, but Einstein was unyielding. He hoped that his friends understood that he could no longer live with Mileva. When she began to feel better, Einstein was relieved.

"The international catastrophe weighs heavily on me as an internationalist person. . . . If only somewhere there was an island for the benign and prudent! There I too would be a fervent patriot."

—Albert Einstein

To take his mind off his family problems, Einstein made a visit to Leyden in the fall. He always felt that Lorentz and Ehrenfest understood him better than anyone else, and he desperately yearned to sit and talk with them away from the ravages of war, secluded in a quiet, peaceful place among a gentler humanity than in Berlin. Needless to say, the three men sat and conversed endlessly about Einstein's general theory of relativity.

The trip did wonders for Einstein, but he soon found himself thrust back into the war his return to Germany. The

New Fatherland League had been banned and the German government demanded all energies—from scientists, professors, and laypeople—to be channeled toward one goal: victory in the war. Even Einstein was unable to avoid being part of the melding of science with technology. His contribution was to aid in the design of aircraft wings.

Life in general seemed to be spiraling downward for Einstein during this period. Shortly after he returned from his visit with Lorentz and Ehrenfest, Einstein learned that his old friend, Fredrich Adler, had assassinated the Austrian premier Count Karl Stürgkh and was in prison. By 1917, Einstein was feeling very old for his thirty-eight years. He started developing health problems that ultimately plagued him for the next four years. Years of intense work, poor eating habits, and irregular sleep all took their toll on his health. The war made obtaining food even more difficult, and Einstein had trouble maintaining the diet his doctor prescribed for him. Among the ailments that Einstein struggled with were gallstones, a stomach ulcer, and jaundice. He was also exhausted.

In the summer of 1917, Einstein traveled to see his family, first stopping to see his mother in southern Germany, picking up Hans Albert in Zurich, and then further convalescing at the home of his sister and her husband, Paul Winteler, in Lucerne. When he returned to Berlin in the fall, Einstein moved into an apartment next door to Elsa instead of going back to his own flat. It was lucky for Einstein that Elsa Lowenthal and her two daughters were part of his life, for they took over caring for him.

Professor Rudolf Ehrmann, a stomach specialist and medical director at Neukölln Hospital, eventually took charge of Einstein's primary medical care. Their initial doctor-patient relationship developed into a friendship that lasted for the rest of Einstein's life. One thing Ehrnman quickly learned about his famous patient was that despite his fondness and respect for doctors, Einstein had little faith in the field of medicine. Einstein was quoted as saying, "the only diagnoses in which I have confidence are those *post mortem*—otherwise none."[8]

Amid all the difficulties swirling around Einstein's life—family problems, illness, the war—the years 1915 through 1917 were among the greatest periods of professional achievement in his life. His ability to insulate himself from distractions had long been a hallmark of his personality, and it served him well while he was working through perhaps the most important scientific theory of the twentieth century. However, even as Einstein continued to convalesce, he felt burned out. In a letter to Zangger after an acute attack towards the end of 1917 that led to his diagnosis of having a duodenal ulcer, he wrote, "Anything really new is invented only in one's youth. Later one becomes more experienced, more famous—and more stupid."[9]

From his bed, Einstein continued to write his scientific papers, including one on gravitational waves—a subject anything but stupid or trivial. He fulfilled whatever professional obligations he was able to handle, including overseeing the plans for Max Planck's sixtieth birthday celebration. As president of the German Physical Society, it was Einstein's responsibility, but the success of the party was important to him because of his genuine fondness for Planck, despite their different positions about the war.

Einstein also made one more plea to the sensibilities of

his colleagues about the war. He made his first plea to French writer and fellow pacifist Romain Rolland in a letter in which he wrote, "The people must be shown that it is necessary to show consideration for non-Germans as persons of equal worth, that it is necessary to earn the trust of foreign countries in order to live, that with brute force and perfidy one does not reach the goals one has set oneself."[10]

Also concerned with the need for a plan to reestablish contact with members of the international scientific community at the conclusion of the war, Einstein drafted a manifesto-type document to his German colleagues in the spring of 1918. His overtures received very little support, so Einstein could only wait patiently for the war to end.

Over the summer Einstein, Elsa, and her daughters made a trip to Ahrenshoop, a small fishing village on the Baltic Sea. The relaxation was very therapeutic for Einstein—no telephones, no university obligations, no distractions. He sat on the beach, blissfully cut off from the newspaper's accounting of the world and all its miseries. It was while on this retreat that Einstein developed his affinity for walking about barefoot. Years later in America, Einstein renewed his pleasure in being barefoot, earning him the reference as the "man without socks."

In Zurich, Mileva had finally consented to a divorce, freeing Einstein and Elsa to marry, something they had talked about off and on for the last few years. As part of the divorce settlement, Einstein agreed to give Mileva the monetary award he would receive when he was finally named a Nobel Prize laureate. It was an interesting proposal, considering that Einstein had been nominated numerous times, but had not yet won. However, everyone was in agreement that it would just be a matter of time, and the prize money would be more than sufficient for Mileva and the children to live quite a comfortable life.

By the late fall, it was apparent that the German Reich was collapsing, and the end to the war inevitable. On November 11, 1918, a special to *The New York Times* read: "WITH THE AMERICAN ARMY IN FRANCE, Nov. 11—They stopped fighting at 11 o'clock this morning. In a twinkling, four years of killing and massacre stopped as if God had swept His omnipotent finger across the scene of world carnage and had cried 'Enough.'"[11] Einstein rejoiced over the news. A few days later he wrote to Maja and Paul, "A great thing has happened. To think that I have lived to see it! . . . Here, militarism and the Privy Councillor nonsense have been thoroughly liquidated."[12]

In the midst of the delirium over the collapse of the imperialist/militaristic regime by the Germans who opposed the war, Einstein wanted to issue a word of caution. He knew all too well that one type of tyranny defeated could easily be replaced by another form of tyranny. But he never got the chance to deliver that caution, and sadly saw his fear of such a possibility become a reality within a very short period of time.

With the war over and his health slowly returning, Einstein had reason to feel somewhat optimistic again. With Elsa's accompaniment, Einstein left Berlin in December for Zurich to fulfill his lecture commitments. The year 1919 was to be very important in Einstein's life. In February, he was granted his divorce. On March 14, 1919, he quietly celebrated his fortieth birthday back in

Berlin in the apartment he shared with the Löwenthal women. Elsa, scarcely known outside Einstein's closest confidants, was an attractive woman three years older than Einstein. She was full of energy and enjoyed life, and seemed to handle Einstein's fame and celebrity well. Einstein must have found her a good companion, because just four months after his divorce from Mileva he escorted Elsa to the altar, where the two exchanged wedding vows on June 2, 1919.

Just days before Einstein and Elsa were married, astronomers on two continents were testing his "deflection of light" theory. A solar eclipse was scheduled to occur on May 29. The war had prevented earlier attempts to set up equipment and photograph the eclipse in 1914, but with the world at peace, Arthur Stanley Eddington, British Plumian Professor of Astronomy at Cambridge, and his assistant, E. T. Cottingham, headed for Principe, a tiny island off West Africa. Colleagues Charles Davidson and A. C. D. Crommelin sailed across the Atlantic to Sobral in the northwestern corner of Brazil in South America.

Eddington was initially disheartened on the day of the eclipse as he awoke to a soaking rain. At about 1:30 P.M., he saw a glimpse of the sun and hurriedly began taking photographs. He exposed as many plates of film as he could change during the eclipse while Cottingham timed the exposures. At one point, Eddington became concerned when he noticed some clouds obscuring the stars. Of the sixteen plates shot, only one showed the stars visible in the frame. That was all Eddington needed. After carefully checking the measurements of the starlight deflection in his photograph, Eddington compared the information against

Einstein's. There was a definite displacement of the light. Proof of Einstein's theory that gravity affected light and that starlight did bend as it passed by the sun was captured in the photograph.

The photos from Brazil confirmed what Eddington and Cottingham's photo captured. It had taken from June until mid-September for Einstein to receive confirmation of the success of the British solar eclipse expedition. Once again Einstein seemed to take the news in stride. When he shared the information with one of his doctoral students, who was elated by the news, Einstein is reported to have given a rather matter-of-fact response, simply saying, "I knew all the time that the theory was correct."[13]

Once the news spread across Europe and into America, the physicist who preferred to spend his time alone with his musings had suddenly been thrust into the spotlight. More important to him than fame and celebrity, however, was the satisfaction in knowing that four Englishmen proved a theory developed by a German. Only a few months earlier, no one would have believed that such cooperation between warring nations was possible.

Scientist, Intellectual, and Advocate for Peace

Einstein's general theory of relativity was viewed as man's greatest intellectual achievement. Scientist J. J. Thomson, who discovered electrons, called Einstein's theory "one of the most momentous, if not the most momentous, pronouncements of human thought."[1] Articles about Einstein and his theory appeared in newspapers around the world, including *The London Times* and America's prestigious paper, *The New York Times*. One headline read. "Revolution in Science—New Theory of the Universe—Newton's Ideas Overthrown." Einstein was unfazed by the fuss. He had always asserted that his work was an extension of the work begun by Newton, so to him it was a logical evolution—hardly a revolution at all.

The real truth of the matter was that most people did not even understand what the theory was, although it seemed that everyone wanted to join the wave of excitement over this momentous achievement in science. And it seemed that people everywhere—in cafés, train stations, or standing on street corners—were surprisingly consumed with conversation and debate about whether Einstein's relativity theory was correct. Because of their lack of understanding of the theory of relativity, the press focused on Einstein, and turned him into a "personality."

Suddenly Einstein was famous, and puzzled by the reaction. Many years later, Einstein reflected, "I never understood why the theory of relativity with its concepts and problems so far removed from practical life should for so long have met with a lively, or indeed passionate, resonance among broad circles of the public."[2] Silent film star Charlie Chaplin, who had invited Einstein to a premiere of his film *City Lights*, noted as they were greeted by throngs of fans outside the theater that he was being cheered because people understood him; they cheered Einstein because they did *not* understand him.

Einstein was not the type to let celebrity go to his head. He quickly shifted his attention from the "relativity circus," as he called it, to his family. In January 1920, Einstein's mother, Pauline, who was terminally ill with stomach cancer, moved in with her son. Because their living quarters were so tight, Einstein moved his mother into his study, and moved his work into a small attic room above their top-floor apartment. It was here that Einstein created his working environment. A few of the walls were lined with shelves overflowing with books, scientific journals, and papers; his one wall decoration indulgence—a print of Isaac Newton. This is where Einstein spent most of his time, working, reflecting, writing, and receiving visitors.

Watching his mother's suffering deeply affected Einstein. He found it difficult to concentrate on his work, and spoke to his friends about her terrible pain. Elsa was a great comfort and did what she could to make Pauline as comfortable as possible. Pauline died toward the end of February. Her death left Einstein grief-stricken and dazed. Life beyond his apartment walls was no consolation. Although Germany appeared at peace with the world, political unrest, distrust, anger, and humiliation permeated every facet of life at home.

The war had left Germany in ruin. The country was plagued by large-scale unemployment and inflation. The new Weimar Republic was viewed as the enemy's puppet government. To preserve the myth that their armed forces were invincible, many Germans blamed their defeat in World War I on traitors who had stabbed their soldiers in the back, and the Jews. Beneath the roaring words of rising hatred was the fact that German Jews had been ardent soldiers. A greater percentage of Jews than non-Jews had served in the German military, with twelve thousand losing their lives in battle for the Fatherland.

The huge reparation conditions imposed by the Allied Powers in the Treaty of Versailles were harsh. Many, including Einstein, thought they would be impossible to meet, raising new concerns about Germany's long-term outlook. The fractured political system left Germany vulnerable to the emergence of several extremist groups, including the Communist Party and the National Socialist German Workers Party (later known as the Nazi Party). It did not take much to feed the flame of anti-Semitism, and despite being a non-practicing Jew, Einstein would be subjected to it along with countless other German Jews.

Regardless of the situation in Germany, Einstein was in demand to give lectures on his newly confirmed relativity theory. For the next several months he traveled a great deal. In May, he visited with his friend Paul Ehrenfest at the university of Leyden, the Netherlands. In June, he traveled to Norway and Denmark to deliver lectures, and on his way back to Berlin, he stopped in Copenhagen to give a lecture at the Astronomical Society. He also met Danish physicist Niels Bohr, who had done much groundbreaking work applying Planck's quantum theory to atomic structure.[3]

Back in Berlin, Einstein found himself identifying with his Jewishness more and more. It was, in fact, the non-Jews in Germany that reminded him of his ethnic origins more than his Jewish brethren. He was turned off by the assimilation of German Jews (those Jews who chose integration with their environment), feeling that they held no self-pride or identity, preferring to at least seem German to other Germans in the hopes of being treated like equal members of society. This behavior led Einstein to acknowledge his ethnicity and show more pride in being Jewish. It was not without consequences.

Because Einstein was now so well-known, it was easy to criticize his work. There were those who did so out of professional envy; others did so because they simply did not understand his theory. He became an even easier target for anti-Semitic groups like the National Socialists, who attacked his work because he was a Jew. Einstein grew increasingly uncomfortable in Germany, and was given an opportunity to escape its turmoil for a while when Chaim Weizmann, president of the World Zionist Organization (WZO) extended an invitation to Einstein to take a trip with him to America. The trip was organized as a means to raise money for the Zionist movement and for the construction of the planned Hebrew University in Jerusalem.

Weizman was born in Russia, and worked for England during the war developing explosives for the Royal Navy. Toward the end of the war, he had convinced the British of the need for a Jewish homeland. Ultimately, the British government consented to help create a Jewish state in Palestine. Einstein recognized that he was being asked not for his scientific expertise to make the trip, but rather for his celebrity status, which was sure to draw large crowds to any WZO appearance. Despite the fact that the trip required Einstein to cancel other engagements that conflicted with the trip schedule, including the Solvay Conference in Brussels, he agreed to go. Einstein had come to consider Judaism not a religion, but a "community of destiny."[4]

On April 21, 1921, Albert and Elsa Einstein arrived in New York with Vera and Chaim Weizman aboard the ocean liner *Rotterdam*. A sea of reporters and photographers anxious to get their first glimpse of the famed scientist greeted their arrival. Einstein was asked to briefly explain his relativity theory. In broken English, he playfully replied, "Before, it was believed that if all material things disappeared out of the universe, time and space would remain.

This political cartoon shows Einstein shedding his "wings of pacifism" and taking up the "sword of preparedness." The cartoon ran in the *Brooklyn Eagle* in 1933 after Einstein issued statements calling for civilization to unite against the oppression of Jews in Germany.

According to my new theory of relativity, time and space disappear with material things."[5]

For the next two months, Einstein was introduced to America—its restaurants, neighborhoods, and people. He visited cities including Boston, Chicago, Princeton, and the nation's capital, Washington, D.C., and often made trips back to New York in between city stops. He gave a lecture at Columbia University and several at the City College of New York, met with the President of the United States, Warren G. Harding, and attended a dinner at the National Academy of Sciences. He visited physics professors Robert Millikan and Albert Michelson at the University of Chicago, and helped several students solve problems during a visit to Harvard.

Although most people found Einstein to be a friendly, down-to-earth fellow who rarely said anything controversial, he did raise a few eyebrows when he was asked to respond to some comments recently made by inventor Thomas Edison about higher education in America. Edison believed that a liberal arts education was a waste of time, and only colleges that taught facts were worthy of attendance. Einstein disagreed, replying:

> A person doesn't need to go to college to learn facts. He can learn them from books. The value of a liberal arts college education is that it trains the mind to think. And that's something you can't learn from textbooks. If a person had ability, a college education helps develop it.[6]

The trip to America had been an overall pleasant experience for Einstein. He had even gotten a surprise visit from his childhood mentor, Max Talmey. The fund-raising fell well short of the anticipated $4 million target, coming in closer to $1 million. Still, that was enough money to begin building the Hebrew University. On their way back to Berlin, the Einsteins made a stop in England, where Einstein met Prime Minister David Lloyd George, took a trip out to Westminster Abbey, and laid a wreath of flowers on the grave of Isaac Newton.

Einstein was not spending much of his time on scientific work anymore; rather, he continued on the lecture circuit and was being drawn further into the post-war political unrest. During a lecture in France, anti-German sentiment gave rise to concern over Einstein's safety. When he returned to Germany, his colleagues shunned him for speaking in France. On June 24, 1922, the German foreign minister, Walther Rathenau, was shot to death as he rode in an open car. There was little doubt that he had been murdered because he was a Jew. The police told Einstein that he and other influential Jews were on a death list. Colleague Philipp Lenard, by now a zealot German Nationalist, had advocated the killing of Rathenau because of his re-establishing diplomatic relations with Russia after the Soviet revolution and for being a Jew.

Realizing that he could no longer stay in Germany, Einstein cancelled several European lectures and withdrew from any political activities. He escaped the dangerous atmosphere building in Germany by accepting lecture invitations abroad. In late October, Albert and Elsa sailed from Marseilles, France, to Kobe, Japan. On the way, they stopped in ports including Singapore, Hong Kong, and Shanghai. While at sea, Einstein received news that he had finally won the Nobel Prize for Physics.

When the Einsteins arrived in Kobe, they were taken to

the first stop on their lecture tour—Tokyo—where they received the same kind of greeting they had upon their arrival in America. They were given a grand tour of the beautiful Asian city, and Einstein's lectures were planned so that there was plenty of time for rest and relaxation in between. After two weeks in Tokyo, the Einsteins moved on for a four-week tour that included visits to Nagoya and Kyoto. Before their trip ended, the Einsteins went to Fukuoka on the island of Kyushu. On December 29, 1922, the Einsteins bid farewell to Japan. On their way back to Berlin, Einstein had planned a stop in Palestine.

Einstein enjoyed his time in Japan very much. "Japan was wonderful. Refined customs, lively interest in everything, intellectual naivety but good intelligence—a splendid people in a picturesque land."[7] His wonderful memories of this land and its people would be shattered less than twenty-five years later when he saw the devastation caused by the atomic bomb in Hiroshima.

Once in Palestine, Einstein was awestruck at how quickly the pioneer settlement was taking form. The pinnacle of the trip was his participation in the inauguration ceremonies at the future site of Hebrew University on Jerusalem's Mount Scopus. He later planted a tree on Mount Carmel, and then made a stop at Haifa's high school and technical college. The Einsteins departed on February 14, 1923. Later, Einstein, in telling Chaim Weizmann about his visit to Palestine, said, "The difficulties are great, but the mood is confident and the work to be marveled at."[8]

After the Einsteins returned to Berlin from their six-month hiatus, Albert was given his Nobel Medal and diploma. Einstein decided to use the Prize money to purchase three homes on the Zürichberg with the intent of renting them out. The income from the rentals would go to Mileva and the children, finally providing them with financial security. That summer, Einstein traveled to Sweden to give his required laureate speech. Back in Berlin, the smear campaign against him continued. Several papers reported that Einstein was going to visit Soviet Russia in the fall. Aside from the rabid hatred of Jews in Germany, they also despised the dreaded communist Bolsheviks.

"A person doesn't need to go to college to learn facts. . . . The value of a liberal arts college education is that it trains the mind to think."

—Albert Einstein

Einstein was actually getting ready to make his yearly visit to Leyden, Holland. He always looked forward to his time there, staying with his good friends the Ehrenfests. It was comfortable, intellectually stimulating, and free of the negative external forces taking place in other parts of the world. While in Leyden, Einstein learned of Adolf Hitler's failed coup at a Munich beer hall. Hitler was later arrested and sentenced to five years in prison. Many hoped that this event would weaken the Nazi Party and they would become an insignificant factor in Germany's politics.

Einstein spent most of 1924 in Berlin, again working on quantum theory. In 1925, he wrote a paper entitled the *Quantum Theory of Single Atom Ideal Gases*. While mulling over quantum theory, he received a manuscript from a young physicist from India named Satyenda Bose. In it, Bose suggested that one should think of photons, or units of light, as particles. Einstein thought a great deal about this wave-particle concept of light. If it was true, then light waves could also be discussed in terms of particles. Einstein theorized that the reverse then should also be true—light particles could be described in terms of waves. From this, Einstein formulated the Bose-Einstein statistics, and published a paper about it toward the end of the year. These discoveries were the last indisputable works of major importance for Einstein.

The restless physicist continued to stay involved in the lecture circuit and kept an interest in the development of Hebrew University. Einstein traveled to South America, worked as a consultant on patent issues, became involved with the League of Nations (the forerunner of the world peace-keeping body the United Nations), and agreed to join the administrative council of Hebrew University. He attended the Solvay Congress in Brussels, where he and Niels Bohr began a long-running debate over the foundations of quantum mechanics. Bohr, along with a colleague Werner Heisenberg, contended that by measuring particles it changes them so as to make it impossible to predict their precise behavior. Einstein rejected the idea that there could be any uncertainty in quantum theory, prompting him to voice his now famous remark, "God does not play dice with the universe."[9]

Einstein's multiple activities allowed for little rest, and years of neglecting his health finally caught up with him. In March 1928 while in Davos, Switzerland, to give a lecture, Einstein collapsed. Although he had not had a heart attack, he was diagnosed with acute inflammation of the walls of his heart. He was put on a strict salt-free diet, indefinite bed rest, and was forbidden to smoke his beloved pipe. To recuperate, Einstein settled in a house in Scharbeutz, a small seaside resort on the Baltic coast not far from Hamburg, Germany. His convalescence was slow and took many months. During that time Elsa hired a secretary, Helen Dukas, to help her husband with his correspondence. She remained in his employ for the next twenty-seven years.

Almost completely recovered by the arrival of his fiftieth birthday on March 14, 1929, Einstein was deluged with telegrams, cards, and gifts, which included a 215-square-foot dinghy cruiser purchased by a group of friends, and an offer by the Berlin city council to select a piece of land on which to build a waterfront house. Although complications prevented that from taking place, the Einsteins decided to buy their own patch of ground and have a home built. They selected the village of Caputh, just south of Potsdam. The Einsteins would spend much time there, with Einstein sailing in his sailboat, which he named the *Tümmler* ("Porpoise").

Despite the idyllic environment in Caputh, Einstein was well aware of the growing political threat in the country. Adolf Hitler had been released from prison after serving only nine months of his sentence. While incarcerated, he had written his memoir called *Mein Kampf*. The book was filled with racist, hateful ideology, in which Hitler described how Germans could seize control and assume their role as the master race of the world. Hitler's vision included a "cleansing" of non-Aryans, including communists and Jews. With Hitler's guidance the Nazi Party was steadily gaining power, and when the Great Depression hit in 1929, they gained support of the millions of Germans who were out of work, with no money and little food to survive.

ALBERT EINSTEIN RELAXES WHILE TAKING HIS BOAT FOR A SAIL.

The Nazi Party members began a campaign of violence and intimidation, first to scare undesirables to flee the country, or deportation to remove those who remained. Einstein, because of his ethnicity and his pacifism, was marked as an enemy of Germany. Aware of the potential danger, Einstein continued to travel abroad to deliver lectures. In 1930, he had finally developed a connection to America, giving a few lectures at the California Institute of Technology (Caltech) in Pasadena. The Einsteins remained in Pasadena as the guests of physicist Robert Millikan through the winter of 1930–1931.

Back in Germany, Einstein spent as little time as possible in Berlin, preferring the quiet and safer environment in Caputh. But it was only a matter of time before the Nazi hatred would wind its way to the seaside village. After packing to go to Caltech for the winter in 1932, Einstein told Elsa to take one last look at their beloved home, because he was certain they would never see it again. As predicted, members of the Nazi Party made their way to Caputh and broke into the Einstein home on the pretense of looking for guns and ammunition they were sure were stored there to be used in a Communist revolt. The money in the Einsteins' bank account in Berlin was confiscated, and their home was also ransacked.

News of the Nazi violations reached the Einsteins while they were sailing back to Germany from America. When the ship docked in Antwerp, Belgium, Einstein decided that he would not return to Germany. He released the following statement:

> These acts are the result of the government's overnight transfer of police powers to a raw and rabid mob of the

> Nazi militia. My summer home has often in the past been honored by the presence of guests. . . . No one had any reason to break in.[10]

Hitler consolidated his power in January by being named chancellor of Germany. In March, after calling for a special election, Hitler's Nazi Party won a majority in the Reichstag (German Parliament) and Hitler named himself Führer, seizing absolute power. Thus began a swift campaign to rid Germany of all non-Aryans, by intimidation, violence, destruction of property, and murder.

The Einsteins took refuge in Le Coq-sur-Mer, Belgium. Unknown to many of his friends and colleagues, Einstein had not been caught off guard while abroad. He had made provisions. His family and secretary, Helen Dukas, made it out of Germany. Whatever was not seized by the Nazis, including some of his more important papers, were delivered to him through the help of French ambassador André Francois-Poncet. From there, Einstein had everything sent on to the United States. Taking care of unfinished German business, Einstein resigned from the Prussian Academy.

The famous professor in exile was recruited by many institutions—the Sorbonne in Paris, Hebrew University in Jerusalem, the University of Madrid, and Caltech in America. However, Einstein had set his mind on Princeton University in New Jersey. During one of his winter stays at Caltech, Einstein was visited by Abraham Flexner. Einstein had previously made Flexner's acquaintance in Pasadena and Oxford. Flexner came to see Einstein to discuss the concept of a new institution designed for advanced study in Princeton. Flexner explained that the idea was to bring on board scientists from all over the world to live on campus where they could continue their research work without any other obligations. Originally, Einstein accepted on condition that he be able to spend six months each year at the University of Berlin, but now that was no longer an issue.

Before leaving for America, Einstein first wanted to make one last trip to Zurich to see his younger son, Eduard, who had suffered a nervous breakdown in 1930. Sadly, Eduard would spend the rest of his life requiring mental therapy. In October, Einstein, Elsa, and Helen Dukas boarded the ship *Westernland* and sailed to New York. Elsa's daughters, Ilse and Margot, remained in Europe. To avoid the horde of press that would no doubt wait for Einstein to emerge, Flexner had arranged for the trio to be taken on a small launch across the harbor to New Jersey. From there, they stayed at a hotel until Elsa found an apartment. Within six months, the wandering scientist from Europe felt comfortable in his new environment, one that would remain his refuge for the last twenty-three years of his life.

Although Einstein's health had not been a problem, he would have to deal with that of his family. In the spring of 1934, Elsa learned that daughter Ilse, who was now in Paris, had become gravely ill. Although Margot was with her, Elsa traveled back to Europe alone to be with them. Unfortunately, Ilse had cancer, and succumbed to the disease in July. Elsa was devastated and never really recovered from the loss.

The following summer, a house across the street from the Einsteins' apartment went up for sale. They decided to buy it, and Elsa supervised the desired renovations while her husband was off sailing. Not long after they moved in, Elsa herself became ill. She developed a swelling around one of her eyes, later diagnosed as a sign of kidney and circulatory problems. She continued to get worse, and died in their Princeton home on December 20, 1936. Einstein never really displayed much grief, but then he was never one to reveal his emotions outwardly.

Without Elsa, Einstein buried himself in his scientific work. His lifelong quest was "to bring the principles of quantum mechanics together with relativity in a unified field theory."[11] While he pondered that, other physicists, including those in Germany, were working on experiments to split atomic nuclei. Lise Meitner, a former student of Max Planck, had concluded that splitting an atom of uranium could release a tremendous amount of energy. She passed the information on to Niels Bohr, who presented the discovery at a conference in Washington, D.C., in early 1939.

This scientific work had military ramifications. Could Germany be possibly trying to develop an atomic bomb? The largest source of uranium was in Zaïre, Africa, a Belgian territory. If Hitler invaded Belgium, he would have easy access to the material. When colleague Leo Szilard brought this to Einstein's attention, a letter was drafted to President Franklin D. Roosevelt to advise him of the concern. It was co-signed by Einstein. On September 1, 1939, German forces invaded Poland. Within a month, other European countries were drawn into battle. World War II had begun.

After reading Szilard's letter, Roosevelt gathered a group of military representatives and scientists including Szilard, Caltech physicist J. Robert Oppenheimer, and Enrico Fermi to study the possibilities. Hitler's armies continued their march through Europe, with only Great Britain not yet defeated. When the Japanese, who along with Italy were German allies, attacked the U.S. naval base at Pearl Harbor, Hawaii, the U. S. was drawn into the war.

In 1940, Einstein became a citizen of the United States. Although he wanted to help his newly adopted country, Einstein was kept from direct involvement in the United States's development of the bomb. In 1942, from the committee Roosevelt established, was born the Manhattan Project, located in Los Alamos, New Mexico. Eventually, the atomic bomb was perfected, and was dropped on the Japanese cities of Hiroshima (August 6, 1945) and Nagasaki (August 9, 1945), officially ending World War II.

Einstein was excited about the scientific aspect of the development of the bomb, but not its use, and came to regret having written the letter to Roosevelt. Although Einstein had dropped his staunch pacifism in face of the Nazi threat that emerged with Hitler's rise to power, he was still committed to pacifistic ideals. Along with other intellectuals such as Niels Bohr and Bertrand Russell, he strongly opposed nuclear arms development, both in the U.S. and around the world.

Having officially retired from the institute in Princeton in mid-1945, Einstein devoted much of his time educating others about the horrors of using atomic energy as a weapon. Slowly, information reached America about the unspeakable atrocities committed against the Jews and others by the Nazis during the war. Six million Jews had been murdered in death camps and by mobile killing squads over the duration of the war. Einstein was appalled and saddened.

Einstein continued to speak out against the immoralities

ALBERT EINSTEIN ENTERTAINS CAPTAIN GEOFFREY E. SAGE AND LIEUTENANT COMMANDER FREDERICK L. DOUTHIT OF THE U.S. NAVY IN HIS STUDY AT HOME IN PRINCETON IN 1943.

of war—especially nuclear warfare—even as the Cold War was quickly developing between the United States and communist Russia. Because of his pacifist views and outspokenness on the subject, Einstein was labeled a communist sympathizer. Fervent anti-communist Senator Joseph McCarthy led a "witch hunt" for communists in America, ruining many lives and careers in the process.

Chaim Weizmann became the first president of the newly created state of Israel in 1948. Einstein was pleased by the establishment of a homeland for Jews and remained an advocate for its continued development. When Weizmann died in 1952, Einstein was asked to assume the presidency. Although deeply honored, Einstein declined, saying "I lack both the natural aptitude and the experience, to deal properly with people and to exercise official functions."[12]

Einstein's own health had been slowly deteriorating. In 1948, it was discovered that he had an aneurysm in the wall of his abdominal aorta, a major internal blood artery. Eventually it would burst and surgery was not an option. He was saddened by the deaths of his sister Maja in 1951, and his old friend Michele Besso, who died the day after Einstein's seventy-sixth birthday. Just a month later, he collapsed at home and was taken to the hospital where it was determined that the aneurysm had a perforation. Einstein refused emergency surgery, saying "I would like to go when I want to. To prolong life artificially is tasteless."[13] He died on April 18, 1955. After his death, Elsa's daughter, Margot, said of her famous step-father:

> He . . . waited for his end as for an impending natural event. Fearless as he had been in life—so quietly and modestly he was facing death. He left this world without sentimentality and without regrets.[14]

Activities

The Principle of Relativity

Einstein's Theory of Relativity is perhaps the most famous principle in modern physics. Although it may seem very complicated, we can see its effects in many of the simplest activities of our everyday lives.

Take a Trip

The next time you are traveling, either by car, plane, or train, wait until the vehicle assumes a steady pace and close your eyes. If the vehicle is moving smoothly, you should not be able to tell you are moving, even though the vehicle is, in fact, moving quite rapidly. Even though the vehicle is moving, you are at rest in your seat.

Now open your eyes and look out the window. What do you see? You will now see objects moving past the window. Because you see objects moving, you now realize you are moving. But *relative* to the vehicle, you are not moving—you remain still in your seat.

Using Your Imagination

Imagine that you are going to a train station with a friend. Your friend stands on the platform some distance from where the train is stopped for passengers to board while you enter the train. Imagine that as the train departs, you roll a ball down the aisle of the train car along the floor in the direction you are moving. Let's say the ball is moving at three yards per second from your point of view.

Your friend watching on the train platform, however,

would see things very differently from his point of view. If he could see inside the train car as it was moving, the ball would appear to be moving much faster to him. Let's say the train was passing through the station at forty yards per second. To your friend, then, the ball would appear to be rolling at a speed of 43 yards per second.

According to Einstein, motion is not the same for each individual. It is *relative* to the observer; therefore, you cannot measure motion and speed without having something to compare it with. To your friend the ball is moving at the speed of the train *plus* the speed of the ball. To you, the ball is only moving at the speed away from you regardless of how fast the train is moving.

CHRONOLOGY

1879—*March 14*: Albert Einstein is born in Ulm.

1895—Leaves school in Germany to join his family now living in Milan.

1896—After finishing high school in Aarau, Switzerland, enrolls at ETH.

1900—Graduates from ETH, but has difficulty finding a job.

1901—Granted Swiss citizenship.

1902—Begins working at the Swiss Patent Office in Bern.

1903—*January 6*: Marries ETH classmate Mileva Maric.

1904—*May 14*: Son Hans Albert is born.

1905—Writes four papers including one on the photoelectric effect and the theory of relativity.

1910—*July 28*: Son Eduard is born.

1914—Einstein takes a post at Berlin University.
World War I breaks out.
Separates from Mileva.

1919—*May 29*: Solar eclipse on confirms the deflection of light in a gravitational field.
June 2: Marries Elsa.

1922—Awarded the Nobel Prize in Physics.

1933—Nazis seize power.

September: Sails for America, never to return to Germany.

1936—*December 20*: Elsa Einstein dies.

1939—Signs a letter to U.S. President Roosevelt in which he refers to the possibility of building an atomic bomb.
September 1: World war II begins in Europe with Germany's attack on Poland.

1940—Becomes an American citizen.

1948—Diagnosed with an aneurysm of the abdominal aorta.

1951—Sister, Maja, dies.

1952—Offered the presidency of Israel, but declines.

1955—*April 18*: Dies three days after his abdominal aneurysm ruptures.

Chapter Notes

Chapter One. The Prize

1. Denis Brian, *Einstein, A Life* (New York: John Wiley and Sons, Inc., 1996), p. 111.
2. Ibid., p. 144.
3. "The Nobel Prize in Physics 1921," *Nobel e-Museum*, June 23, 2003, <http://www.nobel.se/physics/laureates/1921/press.html> (June 27, 2003).
4. Albrecht Fölsing, *Albert Einstein* (New York: Penguin Books, 1997), p. 145.

Chapter Two. An Unremarkable Youth

1. Denis Brian, *Einstein, A Life* (New York: John Wiley and Sons, Inc., 1996), p. 1.
2. John B. Severance, *Einstein: Visionary Scientist* (New York: Clarion Books, 1999), p. 20.
3. Albrecht Fölsing, *Albert Einstein* (New York: Penguin Books, 1997), p. 26.
4. Ibid., p. 16.
5. Severance, p. 21.
6. Brian, p. 4.
7. Fölsing, p. 24.

Chapter Three. An Oasis In Europe

1. Albrecht Fölsing, *Albert Einstein* (New York: Penguin Books, 1997), p. 34.
2. Ibid.
3. Ibid., p. 37.
4. Denis Brian, *Einstein, A Life* (New York: John Wiley and Sons, Inc., 1996), p. 9.
5. Ibid., p. 12.
6. Fölsing, p. 40.
7. Ibid., p. 45.

8. Ibid., p. 48.
9. Ibid., p. 53.
10. Brian, p. 18.
11. Ibid.
12. Ronald W. Clark, *Einstein: The Life and Times* (New York: Avon Books, 1972), p. 54.
13. John B. Severance, *Einstein: Visionary Scientist* (New York: Clarion Books, 1999), p. 32.

Chapter Four. A Tenuous Start for an Improbable Genius

1. Denis Brian, *Einstein, A Life* (New York: John Wiley and Sons, Inc., 1996), p. 31.
2. Ibid., p. 30.
3. Albrecht Fölsing, *Albert Einstein* (New York: Penguin Books, 1997), p. 80.
4. Ibid., p. 85.
5. Ibid., p. 84.
6. Ibid.
7. Ronald W. Clark, *Einstein: The Life and Times* (New York: Avon Books, 1972), p. 68.
8. Fölsing, p. 96.
9. Ibid., p. 96.
10. Clark, p. 81.
11. Fölsing, p. 101.
12. Ibid., p. 103.
13. Ibid.
14. Ibid., p. 102.
15. Clark, p. 73.
16. Brian, p. 53.

Chapter Five. The Miracle Year of 1905

1. Albrecht Fölsing, *Albert Einstein* (New York: Penguin Books, 1997), p. 105.

2. "The Great Works I," *Einstein-Image and Impact-AIP History Center Exhibit*, n.d., <http://www.aip.org/history/einstein/great1.htm> (June 27, 2003).

3. Fölsing, p. 121.

4. Ronald W. Clark, *Einstein: The Life and Times* (New York: Avon Books, 1972), p. 87.

5. Robert Cwiklik, *Albert Einstein and the Theory of Relativity* (New York: Barrons, 1987), p. 76.

6. "Einstein, Albert," *Britannica Guide to the Nobel Prizes*, 1997, <http://www.britannica.com/nobel/macro/5002_5.html> (June 27, 2003).

7. Fölsing, p. 116.

8. Denis Brian, *Einstein, A Life* (New York: John Wiley and Sons, Inc., 1996), p. 61.

9. Fölsing, p. 155.

10. Ibid., p. 123.

11. Brian, p. 28.

12. Cwiklik, p. 97.

13. Fölsing, p. 201.

Chapter Six. Among the Scientific Elite

1. Albrecht Fölsing, *Albert Einstein* (New York: Penguin Books, 1997), p. 221.

2. Denis Brian, *Einstein, A Life* (New York: John Wiley and Sons, Inc., 1996), p. 72.

3. Fölsing, p. 247.

4. Ibid., p. 251.

5. Brian, p. 75.

6. Fölsing, p. 256.

7. Ibid., p. 257.

8. Ibid., p. 259.

9. *Max-Planck-Institut für Gravitationsphysik (Albert-Einstein-Institut)*, May 1, 2000, <http://auriga.astro.physik.uni-potsdam.de/~afeld/einstein/einstein.html> (June 27, 2003).

10. Fölsing, p. 276.
11. Ibid., p. 280.
12. Ibid., p. 327.
13. Ibid., p. 330.

Chapter Seven. An Outsider in Berlin

1. Albrecht Fölsing, *Albert Einstein* (New York: Penguin Books, 1997), p. 335.
2. Ronald W. Clark, *Einstein: The Life and Times* (New York: Avon Books, 1972), p. 228.
3. Ibid., p. 229.
4. Denis Brian, *Einstein, A Life* (New York: John Wiley and Sons, Inc., 1996), p. 90.
5. Fölsing, p. 347.
6. John B. Severance, *Einstein: Visionary Scientist* (New York: Clarion Books, 1999), p. 60.
7. Brian, p. 91.
8. Fölsing, p. 418.
9. Ibid., p. 412.
10. Ibid., p. 414.
11. Edwin L. James, "The New York Times Reports the End of the War," *The World War I Document Archive*, September 11, 1918, <http://www.lib.byu.edu/~rdh/wwi/1918/nytend.html> (June 27, 2003).
12. Fölsing, p. 422.
13. Ibid., p. 439.

Chapter Eight. Scientist, Intellectual, and Advocate for Peace

1. Albrecht Fölsing, *Albert Einstein* (New York: Penguin Books, 1997), p. 445.
2. Ibid., p. 457.
3. John B. Severance, *Einstein: Visionary Scientist* (New York: Clarion Books, 1999), p. 68.
4. Fölsing, p. 491.

5. Denis Brian, *Einstein, A Life* (New York: John Wiley and Sons, Inc., 1996), p. 120.
6. Ibid., pp. 129–130.
7. Fölsing, p. 528.
8. Brian, p. 145.
9. Severance, p. 85.
10. Ibid., p. 95.
11. Ibid., p. 108.
12. Ibid., p. 121.
13. Fölsing, p. 740.
14. Ibid., p. 741.

Glossary

absolute—Free of limits or requirements.

academic—Relating to school or college.

advocate—A person who argues for, recommends, or supports another person's cause.

algebra—A branch of mathematics that explores the relationships between numbers and the operations used to work with them. Algebra uses letters or other symbols to represent these relationships.

assimilate—To take something in and make it part of the thing it has joined.

astronomy—The science of the heavenly bodies and of their sizes, motions, and makeup.

atom—The smallest particle of an element that has the properties of the element.

chemistry—A science that deals with the makeup, structure, and properties of substances and with the changes that they go through.

citizenship—Having the rights and privileges of a citizen.

controversial—Creating or causing long or heated discussions of a subject about which people have many different opinions.

discrimination—The act of treating some people better or worse than others without any fair or proper reason.

doctorate—The degree, title, or rank of a doctor.

electron—A particle of an atom that has a negative charge of electricity and travels around the nucleus of an atom.

engineer—A designer or builder of engines, or a person who is trained in or follows a branch of engineering as a career.

entrepreneur—A person who organizes, manages, and assumes the risks of a business.

envoy—A representative sent by one government to another.

ethnicity—The state of being related to a race or large group of people classed according to common traits and customs.

fluctuation—The state of constantly moving up and down or back and forth like a wave.

geometry—A branch of mathematics that deals with points, lines, angles, surfaces, and solids.

gravitation—A force of attraction that tends to draw particles or bodies of matter together.

kosher—Accepted by Jewish law.

laureate—A person honored for achievement in an art or science.

mass—A quantity of matter that clings together in one body.

molecule—The smallest particle of a substance that has all the characteristics of the substance.

nominate—To choose as a candidate for an election, appointment, or honor.

patent—A writing that grants an inventor the only right to make, use, or sell his or her invention for a term of years.

phenomenon—A fact, feature, or event of scientific interest.

philanthropist—A person who actively tries to promote human welfare and goodwill.

physics—A science that deals with matter and energy and their actions upon each other.

physiology—A branch of biology that deals with the processes and activities by which life is carried on in living things.

polarize—To cause to vibrate (as light waves) in a definite pattern and in opposite groups.

prejudice—Unfriendly feelings directed against an individual, group, or race.

radar—A device that sends out radio waves for detecting and locating an object by reflecting radio waves. The reflection of these waves is used to find the position and speed of the object.

silica—A compound that consists of silicon dioxide and that is found in quartz, opal, and sand.

solar eclipse—The total or partial hiding of the sun by the moon.

synagogue—A house of worship for Jewish people.

theoretical—Existing only as a general idea or principle.

thesis—A statement put forth for discussion or proof.

velocity—Speed; quickness of motion.

volatile—Likely to change suddenly or quickly. In science, a volatile substance is one that becomes a vapor at a very low temperature.

Further Reading

Bankston, John. *Albert Einstein and the Theory of Relativity.* Bear, Del.: Mitchell Lane Publishers, 2000.

Heinrichs, Ann. *Albert Einstein.* Milwaukee, Wis.: Gareth Stevens, Inc., 2002.

MacDonald, Fiona. *Albert Einstein: The Genius Behind the Theory of Relativity*. Farmington Hills, Mich.: Gale Group, 2000.

Macleod, Elizabeth. *Albert Einstein: A Life of Genius.* Buffalo, N.Y.: Kids Can Press, 2003.

Pasachoff, Naomi. *Niels Bohr: Physicist and Humanitarian.* Berkeley Heights, N.J.: Enslow Publishers, Inc., 2003.

Reid, Struan. *Albert Einstein.* Chicago: Heinemann Library, 2001.

Internet Addresses

Albert Einstein Home Page
http://www.humboldt1.com/~gralsto/einstein/einstein.html

Einstein: Person of the Century & Other Links
http://leiwen.tripod.com/pocstory.htm

Nobel Prize Home Page
http://www.nobel.se/

INDEX